JOE HUBER: WINNING WITH FAMILY

JOE HUBER:
WINNING
WITH
FAMILY

BY JOE HUBER

WITH BRAD WATSON AND ERIC WRIGHT

STRAWBERRY PRESS

Joe Huber: Winning with Family.

Edited, designed, and produced by Barrett Shaw.

For information write to:
Strawberry Press, Inc.
P.O. Box 448, Jeffersonville, IN 47131.

ISBN 0-9647275-0-1

Library of Congress Catalog Card Number: 95-069471

Contents

Recipes

My parents, Joseph and Mary Koetter Huber.

Dedication

I was nineteen years old, and Mother decided I needed a spanking. I laughed, "You're kidding!" "No," Mom said, "I'm serious!" I responded, "Mother, I'm nineteen years old, you can't spank me." "Well, of course I can spank you," she hollered, "lay across that kitchen table!" Just as calmly as I could reply, I said, "Well, Mother, I know we have a disagreement here, and I know I need to be disciplined, but, by gosh, I'm nineteen years old. You can't spank me!" One more time she answered, "I can spank you and I'm going to. Now you lay across that kitchen table." So, I laid across that kitchen table and she proceeded to take her hand and paddle my butt. I just couldn't help it, though; I got so tickled that I started laughing, and I mean I was laughing hard. Well, she ended up laughing and laying on the side of the table right with me, and I believe that that was one of the best laughs that my mother and I ever had together, getting a spanking when I was nineteen years old. Funny thing is, still today I have no idea what I did to deserve it.

Another wonderful experience for me was when we built our first company picnic building in 1990. The very first party we had in that building was for my mother's 90th birthday. We invited the whole community and friends of hers from Kansas. Everybody we could think of, we invited, and over six hundred people showed up. During the party, all of her grandchildren and great-grandchildren walked up on the stage we have in there carrying long-stemmed red roses, and we ended up giving Mother ninety roses for her birthday. For Mother to watch all of her grandchildren and great-grandchildren carry those roses up to her was a super experience for her and everybody else that was there.

My mother also played the organ and sang in our church for over sixty years. One of her favorite songs was called "On This Day, Oh Beautiful Mother," and I had asked Mother a couple of weeks before, when we were planning this birthday party, if she would play and sing that song. She said, "Oh, Junior, you know, my eyes are getting pretty bad, and I really can't see the notes, but if you find somebody to play it, I can sure sing it!" So, I had a friend of mine come in, and we moved a piano up there for him to play. That day, Mother got on the microphone and she threw her head back and she sang that song as well as I had ever heard her sing it in my life. Ninety years old! She was jerking tears out of that crowd like you wouldn't believe, and when she finished, she made this statement: "Before you can do anything, you have to want to do it, and I sure wanted to do this."

My dad, on the other hand, wasn't so gentle when it came to getting his message across. I can remember he always used to ask me, "Why do I always have to kick you in the *butt* to get it in your *head?*" The thing he always taught us was responsibility. My dad's sense of responsibility was unbelievable. He stayed here on the farm with his mother until he was twenty-nine years old to help her take care of their family. Now, *that's* responsibility.

I can also remember, though, how gentle he could be whenever Bonnie was around. When we were buying the farm, he could tell that Bonnie was very nervous about our future, and — I'll never forget — he walked up to her and said, "Don't worry, you'll always make a little bit of money." And you know what? He was right. Even during our first few years on the farm when a monster hail came down and took just about everything with it, we made just enough to get by.

During the later years of his life when he had emphysema so bad that he could hardly get around, he'd walk with his cane from the house, across the road, almost over to the next farm to be close to Bonnie as she was helping out in the fields. In our hearts, we know that the only reason he did that was to let her know how much he appreciated her help. He appreciated it, and because we appreciate everything that my mother and dad have done for us, Bonnie and I would like to dedicate this book, to them.

"For Mother and Dad,
whose lives touched
so many."

Anna Faske Huber — Grandma Huber.

1

Foundations

M y Grandma Huber always gave the impression that "You can do anything" if you put your mind to the task. She believed in this saying and passed it on to all her children. All of Grandma Huber's children believed they could do anything, and this showed in the things they accomplished in their lives. They became the leaders in the community of Starlight, and each child excelled in whatever he or she was involved with.

My Uncle Ignatius, Nace was his nickname, married my Aunt Bertha and they had seven children. Uncle Nace worked with my Uncle Bill at a mill in Greenville. Bill and Nace would haul the flour to Louisville where bread was baked, drop it off, and pick up bread to take to Evansville. Unfortunately, their mill had a fire and it shut down. Nace did not want to go back to the farm so he, Uncle Bill and Uncle Louis, Skinny was his nickname, started a trucking company, Huber and Huber Motor Express. Nace was President and really put a great deal of time into the company. It started off with only one truck and just a few routes. However, Huber and Huber became a success within just a few years. They had nineteen terminals throughout the Central United States. These terminals would have freight delivered and then they would ship to local businesses in these communities. Routes were in big cities such as Indianapolis, Atlanta, Knoxville, Cincinnati, and Chicago. Trucks made runs throughout the day delivering freight, and soon Huber and Huber had 1,300 semis on the road. Now, Huber and Huber was not the only company that Nace started. In 1938, he also founded Huber Tire Company, which is still in existence today. This company is currently being managed by Hubers of today's generation.

My Uncle Bill was the Vice President of Huber and Huber with Nace, and he really enjoyed working and seeing the company grow. He married my Aunt Mary and they had four children. My Uncle Bill wanted to start a company that depended upon the land so that he could pass it on to his sons, so he bought two hundred acres, and that soon grew to eight hundred. Then in 1939 Uncle Bill founded Huber Sod Nursery, which is still a family enterprise today.

My Aunt Cecila and Aunt Agnes both married very prominent men. Cecila married John Book, a neighbor who was in the dairy business. Uncle Johnny really enjoyed politics and served as precinct committee chairman for many years. They had three children. Aunt Agnes, whose nickname was Nick, married Herman Gettelfinger who was a very prominent businessman. Uncle Herman and Aunt Agnes were a fun-loving couple, and laughter to them was as natural as breathing. I always remember Uncle Herman in the kitchen with his sisters-in-law, saying "Chicken and dumplings are better the second day." They moved to Knoxville and Herman started Blue Gray Truck Lines, which was a well known trucking company. Later, the family started Kelso Oil Company, which specialized in home delivery of oil. They had five children. Kelso Oil Company is still a family business today.

My Aunt Rosalene decideded to stay around to help out with Huber and Huber Motor Express. Aunt Rosalene never married and lived out her career as the bookkeeper for Huber and Huber. Aunt Rosalene was a very special lady. She would never forget the birthdays of her fifty-three nieces and nephews, and she was like our second mother. She often had the nieces and nephews live with her while they went to school at Bellarmine or if they just needed a place to stay. Grandma Huber lived with Aunt Rosalene till she passed away.

My Uncle Edward stayed in Starlight and did very well as a fruit and vegetable farmer. He married Philomena Stumler, who was part of the family that started the Stumler tradition in Starlight. They had five children. I remember my Uncle Edward as the person who was always giving a helping hand when it was needed. He would go out of his way to help the folks and to make Starlight a better place to live.

My Uncle Carl stayed at the "Home Place" and worked the original land of the Huber family. This is where the Huber

Winery and orchard are located today. He married Marcella Stumler, who also was part of the prominent Stumler family of Starlight. Uncle Carl and Aunt Marcella had eight children. My Uncle Carl and Aunt Marcella gave the same type of dedication to their children that Grandma Huber gave to hers. They wanted to continue the success of the farm and they certainly have. Uncle Carl passed the farm down the family to Gerald and Carl, who now have passed the farm on to their sons Ted and Greg. The "Home Place" of the Huber family still continues to provide for the generations of the future. The seventh generation of the Hubers are living on the farm today. The "Home Place" has grown from the original eighty acres of land to over five hundred acres.

Then there was my father, Joseph Henry Huber, who stayed on the farm helping my Grandma Huber keep the farm productive. My father married my mother, Mary Koetter, when he was twenty-nine years old. They decided to start a family and they had eleven children: Paul, Charles, Norbert, Rosemary, Doris, Kathryn, Cecilia, Carol, John, David, and myself. He was very committed to farming and creating new products to grow to send to the market in Louisville. My father, along with growing many other fruits and vegetables, was the first person to grow cantaloupes in Starlight. He decided to buy his own farm, and that is where I grew up. I still live in that very house today. I watched my mother and father, and I learned from their dedication to the family as well as to the farm.

One thing that my Grandma Huber definitely gave to my father and my aunts and uncles was a sense of "You Can Do It." Therefore, I attribute much of my success to Grandma Huber, my parents, and my aunts and uncles. "You Can Do It," "You Can Do It"!!!

The entire Huber family has found success in one form or another, and our motivation and drive came from Grandma Huber. But how, one might ask, did she accomplish that?

A new land

To begin this story, I must look back to the days of my Great-Great Grandfather Simon Huber. Simon was the Huber that started our generations here in America. He was born in Baden, Germany, in 1794. Simon and his wife Gertrude and their children immigrated to the United States around 1835, and in

3

1843 they moved to the "Home Place." Part of his decision to move to America was because of the opportunities of the new land, but the main reason was the religious unrest of the Catholic Church in Germany, resulting from the May Laws.

The May Laws were established to force young men to serve in the Germany military. This in turn led many Catholics to leave that area in search of religious freedom without forced military service. The news of America and the freedom of religion was very appealing to immigrants; therefore, my Great-Great Grandfather Simon Huber decided to move west.

When Simon came to America he brought seven apple trees to set up an orchard. The land in Baden, Germany, I hear, is very similar to the land here in Starlight. Simon acquired this property as part of the Homestead Act that allowed settlers to receive a portion of property for a very minimal price. In return, Simon was to develop the land. He found the land in Starlight, Indiana, a great place to produce fruits and vegetables. Starlight is located on top of the knobs, and these knobs with their deep ravines create super air drainage, allowing the growing seasons to be three to four weeks longer than on the land in the lower valleys. This is where my family, the Huber family, began our tradition of growing fruits and vegetables.

Simon and Gertrude had eight children, all born in Germany. One of their sons was my Great Grandfather Ignatius Huber, who was born in Baden in 1823. He was four years old when he came to Indiana. He married Maria Ast and they had seven children. Their sixth child was my Grandfather, Charles; but more on that later.

The times on the farm

I remember hearing that the average day, during that time, was very long. The children would get up and do their morning chores. Most of the chores outside were done by the boys, and the girls would stay inside and do most of the housework. They did all the things that were necessary to survive. That was the key during this time, survival, and the only way to survive was to live off the farm. The fields were planted with a variety of vegetables and fruits in the gardens and orchards. These vegetables were then canned so they would have food during the winter months. Often, they would can two hundred half

4

gallons of green beans during the summer! The girls stayed inside the house baking bread and washing clothes on a washboard because they did not have the luxury of electricity. They also had to be good cooks because they had to feed the entire family. The boys, in turn, would run the farm by feeding the livestock, which usually consisted of cattle and pigs, and by doing many of the other farming jobs. The cattle were milked every morning and every evening, and it was important that the cows were milked by the same person consistently because they produced more milk from a familiar hand. The pigs had to be fed and fattened so they could be slaughtered for meat. The boys also had to know how to use a team of mules so they could plow the fields, because in these times mules were your tractor. In the winter, it was very important to keep wood cut so there could be heat in the home. Needless to say, the work on the farm was always very long: from dawn to dusk.

The children did go to school, but they usually did not attend past the eighth grade. This was because they were needed to do much of the work around the farm. The children walked to St. John's School, which was about one-and-a-half miles from their home. During bad weather, they would sometimes ride to school in a covered wagon for protection against the elements. There was a stable at St. John's and those neighbors close by would feed the horses with their hay and straw. My Aunt Marcella told me that the children were taught very well, because their teachers were Benedictine nuns who were well educated. These nuns would not tolerate bad behavior; if you caused a problem you were spanked and sent home, which meant you'd probably be spanked by your parents as well. Sometimes, you were spanked if you had not learned the lesson being taught that day! So, it was smarter to pay attention in the first place and avoid a spanking altogether.

The social life revolved around the church and the neighbors. The church was the place where people went to see other people, because it was not only a place of worship, it was a place for people to socialize. It was very unlikely for someone not to attend church regularly. The story, according to my sister Rosemary, was that Anna Faske (Grandma Huber) used to wait for Charles Huber (Grandpa Huber) after Mass was over to make sure that he noticed her. She would often stay after church just for a chance to see him. Eventually, her persistence paid off and she and Charles began a relationship.

Beginning the heritage

Anna Faske married Charles Huber and eventually became known as Grandma Huber. She passed on many of her values to our family throughout all the generations. Grandma Huber was born in Covington, Kentucky, and her family, the Faskes, migrated to Clark County, Indiana, near the "Home Place" of the Huber family.

Charles and Anna decided to marry in 1891 and they wanted to continue working the land at the "Home Place." They decided to plant strawberries along with many vegetables in the fields, and Charles also wanted to keep an orchard with peaches, apples, and other fruit trees. In addition, Grandpa wanted to have grapevines to produce wine and jellies. Grandpa and Grandma Huber were determined to make the farm a success.

Soon after their marriage, they decided to start a family. They sure did start a family, because they ended up with nine children within a sixteen-year period. The oldest was Uncle Ignatius and the youngest was Uncle Carl. The girls were, from oldest to youngest: Aunt Cecilia, Aunt Rosalena, and Aunt Agnes. The boys were, from oldest to youngest: Uncle Ignatius, Uncle William, my dad Joseph, Uncle Edward, Uncle Louis, and Uncle Carl.

My father and my aunts and uncles worked very hard to keep the farm moving, but there were some times when they could have some fun. I remember them telling me how they would play euchre and pinochle late into the night and how they were so competitive. They would play by the light of the kerosene lantern and each one savored the taste of victory. These games would get intense and many say this is where they got their competitive spirit. I remember that my Aunt Marcella said my Uncle Carl bet one million dollars on a game of marbles! The only person that had that kind of money in those days was John D. Rockefeller. Carl was always a betting man and acquired the nickname John D. He even named his first son John D. (Donnie) Huber.

There was also time for them to socialize with the neighbors' children. Occasionally there would be trips into town; however, these trips were few and it was considered a reward to go. I also remember hearing about kitchen dances in those days. These dances would be at someone's home with all the neighbors and the children. Somebody would play an instrument such as fiddle, guitar, or jug. The folks would dance around and laugh while the music was playing. These were the ways that the folks spent their extra time and socialized.

Now, that being said, our family had very little extra time due to their extreme commitment to the family and the farm. The family and the farm were each very much a part of the other. The family depended on the farm to survive. The farm, in turn, had to have the family to make the fruits and vegetables grow. Therefore, it was up to Grandpa and Grandma Huber to keep things moving in the right direction.

Grandpa was a very dedicated farmer during these times. He spent countless hours sowing the fields and planting the fruit and vegetables. He would spend hours trimming the orchards to assure their productivity. He asked that my father and my uncles help with as much of the work on the farm as possible. So, the boys quit school after the eighth grade and would work from early morning to late in the evening, keeping the livestock fed, and caring for the vegetables and fruit trees. They grew to be hard-working young men under the direction of Grandpa and Grandma Huber. Hard work, drive, and commitment were seen in every task they were asked to do. It was also considered rewarding to be asked to take on a new chore around the farm, because responsibility was very important to our family.

The same was true for my aunts. Grandma insisted that they work hard in their daily tasks. She would not let them do a job in a "halfway" manner. They worked cleaning, cooking, sewing, washing, and keeping the house comfortable for the whole family. They were, undoubtedly, a team family with everyone playing a key part. Grandpa and Grandma Huber were the team leaders and they loved and cared dearly for the children and the farm.

Tragedy in the field

In the summer of 1910, Grandpa Huber was working behind the plow to prepare the land for sowing. The sweat must have poured off him in the hot summer day, but he was determined to finish the work he had started because time pressed to get the crops planted. He had started out early in the day and had not taken a break, and suddenly he fell to the ground suffering from a heart attack. Grandpa was quickly taken from the field into the home to be cared for by Grandma. The doctor came to help Grandma but Grandpa's heart was already failing. Grandpa Huber was such a strong man that he struggled for two more days, but eventually his heart just gave up. The family, torn apart by this traumatic loss, was quickly pulled together by Grandma Huber and her commitment.

Grandma Huber — the drive

Grandma Huber could have given up on the children, especially the older boys, but she had such a determination to keep this family together. As time went on, the older boys really had to pick up many of the jobs being done on the farm. Grandma Huber, however, was right out there with the boys doing much of the work on the land to continue making the farm productive. She became very dominant with the children because they needed her strong will to continue. She required the girls to do much more work in the house so that she could be out on the land working from daylight to dusk. This was an extremely hard task because the younger children, especially Uncle Carl, who was two at the death of Grandpa, had to be watched over and cared for.

I remember being told that many of the children, during these times, came down with influenza. Grandma Huber was a midwife in the community and delivered many of the babies in this area. She learned many nursing skills from other women and doctors she associated with. Grandma Huber believed in many home remedies and she had a great deal of success curing sickness with poultices, onion poultice being one of her favorites. Grandma created several different poultices and she used them to help the sick throughout the community. She often would help take care of a neighbor's child so that the parents could continue working.

Influenza really hurt communities in these times and many children died because there was no medication to treat the virus. Grandma Huber would often use camphor salves with a little bit of water to help rid the children of the congestion from the influenza. Many times, one of the young Huber children would have to be cared for because they were sick to the point of death. The children were very lucky to have a mother with her education.

Sickness was not the only hardship that struck the area of Starlight. There were very hard times when the Bank of Borden fell in the Great Depression. Many farmers lost all their money during this period, and it caused many people to give up farming and take to other trades. Even though this did affect the Hubers, it was not going to cause them to sell the farm. They continued to work the land, even though they may not have had all the money they needed to buy the seeds and supplies. Their commitment paid off over time.

Learning what was right and wrong

Grandma Huber had her hands full without Grandpa to help support the family, but I know that she was very committed to teaching the children what was right and wrong. I can remember that Grandma Huber only wanted the right things to be done by her children, and she did not tolerate any wrong. When we were children, Grandma Huber was someone we didn't want to upset because she would make us feel very, very guilty. She led our family by her example, and she would only allow good Christian people under her roof.

Religion was very important to Grandma Huber. The children would often say a blessing before *and* after each meal. This would be done to bless the meal and then to remind them of how thankful they should be following. Along with blessings, the family would read Bible stories from a German Bible before going to bed, and I can remember that during Lent Grandma Huber would have everyone kneel and pray the rosary before bedtime.

The church was also a very important part of Grandma Huber's family. The family went to Mass together every Sunday and then they would return in the evening for Vespers. Grandma instilled the belief that there was so much to be grateful for and that our family's time at church was very important. The children were to wear their finest clothes and were reminded that church was not a place to play and horse around. Grandma Huber was a first-class lady, and she insisted that her children act in a first-class manner.

I'm sure that there were times when Grandma Huber almost gave up while she was working so hard teaching her children right from wrong. So Grandma Huber found a place that she could get away from my father and my aunts and uncles if she needed. Her garden was a place of relaxation, and she would spend countless hours pulling weeds and caring for her beautiful flowers. This was a place where the children knew not to bother her, because she needed to have her time alone. I am thankful that Grandma could find some peace because I am sure that the pressures of the hard times were sometimes overwhelming.

The family spent each meal together and they would have to ask permission to leave the table. Even if one of the children had a date, they did not leave until they had finished dinner with the family. I know that at the dinner table Grandma Huber would have many family talks when things the children had done bothered her. She did not tolerate back talk, but I am sure it occurred because our family has a very competitive spirit and back talk would be inevitable. However, Grandma Huber had a line that did not get crossed and if someone did, they would be punished. If they misbehaved, Grandma Huber spanked my father and the other kids. Sprouts from a maple tree hung in the kitchen for that sole purpose. That was the way it was done, and when I say spanked, I don't mean a light tap. You were spanked hard enough that you didn't want to get into trouble anymore.

I know there had to be times when the children would get into trouble for things such as teasing and family fights, but never really anything that is untypical of brothers and sisters. However, Grandma definitely got her point across to my father and my aunts and uncles about what is right and what is wrong. To my knowledge, there has never been a Huber, throughout all the generations, that has ever been arrested for a felony. Now, that is knowing right from wrong! Grandma Huber emphasized the importance of knowing what is right and what is wrong to all her children and grandchildren every day by her actions. This is something that today's children don't have a clear understanding of. I believe that it is an issue of respect. Grandma Huber understood how each person deserves respect and, therefore, demanded each of her children and grandchildren to give others, along with herself, complete respect always. Grandma has five-hundred-and-thirty-two descendents, and because of her we are the family we have become today.

Recipe:

Grandma's Chicken Dumplings

1 egg	1/4 tsp. salt
1 tsp. water	1 tsp. lard
1 cup flour	fresh parsley or parsley flakes
1/8 tsp. baking powder	chicken broth

Mix dry ingredients and cut in lard. Mix egg with water and combine with flour mixture to make a dough. Roll out and cut in 1-inch squares. Boil in chicken broth about 15 minutes.

Grandpa William Koetter.

2

My Early Life

I guess you could say that I haven't moved around too much. On March 20, 1933, I was born in the same house that I live in today. I grew up here in the Starlight community, and this is the only place that I've ever lived. Some people say that I grew up in the strawberry shed, because when I was two months old my mother would put me in a cradle and take me out with her to the shed so that she could help crate all the strawberries. Maybe that stuck with me all these years; I don't know.

I can also remember that for about three weeks in May, up until the time I was about fourteen years old, my mother and dad would have up to twenty-five kids live in the house with us, and they would help us pick strawberries. My mother would cook and clean for all those children (talk about total commitment), and at the end of the day, if we had really done a good job, my dad would let us ride the truck down to the Fruit Growers Association, where he'd buy us all some ice cream. Strawberries always have been a big part of my life.

Mom and Dad

The greatest assets in my life were my mom, dad, and my five brothers and five sisters. Mom and Dad taught me more about how to live than any school I ever walked into. I learned the importance of responsibility just from being near my father. When my grandfather passed away in 1910, my father stayed on the farm with his mother until he was twenty-nine years old. In 1925, he had finally saved up enough money and bought the farm. Even though he and my mother were seriously

13

contemplating marriage at this time, he worked the farm for another year until he was certain that he could make a living with it. Only after he was sure that he could support a family did he ask my mother to marry him. How many men today show that kind of responsibility?

Dad had a great love for the land, and he understood what God and Mother Nature meant for farm life to be like. He cared for his farm and took care of the land like it was his child. In me, he instilled the responsibility of taking care of the land and the family, and I hope and pray that I can pass on that same responsibility to my children and grandchildren.

My mother instilled in us the desire to broaden the scope of our lives, culturally and musically. Mother learned to play the piano and organ from the Benedictine nuns at St. John's church and school. She played the organ at our church for over sixty years, hundreds of weddings, funerals, and Masses. She loved playing, which was obvious. The memories of Mother playing her piano in our home are some of my most pleasant, especially when she played and sang "Kickety Katie." Mother and Dad taught us kids more than they ever knew they had. What a wonderful family to grow up with!

Early influences

We've already talked about Grandma Huber. Another big influence on my life was my Grandpa Koetter, my mother's dad, who was a true gentleman. I remember that he had a very long mustache that he would meticulously trim. When we were kids, he used to sit at the dining room table with a mirror in one hand, a pair of barber scissors in the other, and snip, snip, snip, snip! Out of ten of those snips maybe one ever touched that mustache. The rest of them were out in the air somewhere; but he couldn't make a miscue on his mustache — it was his pride and joy.

One of the better memories that I have of Grandpa Koetter is from when I was about eleven years old. We were castrating male pigs; not that that's a really great memory in itself, but it just happens to be what we were doing at the time. Anyway, he'd wait until those pigs were about six weeks old, and when they weighed about fifty pounds he would catch them and castrate them. If you didn't do that, when they matured their meat would be so strong that you couldn't eat it.

My job that day was to catch those pigs by their hind legs,

with their bellies toward me, and carry them over to Grandpa Koetter. I'll spare you the details, but you can imagine how those pigs carried on. Well, one of these pigs got to carrying on and kicking so bad that I lost my grip on his legs and he kicked me right in the thigh. Now I'm telling you that when a pig kicks you with those pointy toes it hurts! I lost my temper and said, "G. D." It didn't take me but a second to realize what I'd done.

Grandpa looked up at me and said very calmly, "Turn the pig loose." I was only eleven years old, but that didn't mean I didn't know that I'd better think of something quick. I said, "But you're not done with this pig yet!" Grandpa looked up just as calmly as the first time he'd said it, and reiterated, "Turn the pig loose," all the while wiping off the blade of his pocket knife on his trousers and putting it back in his pocket. "You and me have got to have a talk."

I thought I was really going to get it, but he sat me down on one of the log sills we had in the barn and said, "We don't curse. There's no reason for you to be using God's name in vain. Just because that pig kicked you is no reason for you to holler G. D." We had about a half-hour lecture that day about language, and he made it clear to me that when you're a religious person you don't take God's name in vain. He also made me understand that when people cursed and used slang, it was a sign that they were uneducated, and that I was going to have to learn how to speak if I was going to make it in this world. The image you project and the language you use are all that people recognize you to be. I never, never have forgotten what he told me that day.

Grandpa Koetter's pride

In his older years, his health failed, as everybody's does, but he never used that as an excuse not to do the right thing. At our church, for example, there are ten big steps that lead up from the road, and after about fifty feet, there are ten more steps to climb that lead into the church. Grandpa would be tired after he climbed those steps (in his three-piece suit and felt fedora hat, I might add), but he'd stop and catch his breath before he walked into the church. When he entered that church, he made sure he was upright and ramrod straight. Then, though a lot of the older folks would lean on a bench for support, or just bow their heads as they entered the sanctuary, he'd be as stiff as a board and go all the way down on one knee and touch that floor when he genuflected, and come right back up like he was a twenty-year-old. That's the kind of man he was. Just because he was old didn't make it acceptable to do something half-right. Half-right is just as wrong as all wrong, and Grandpa wasn't about to let anybody think less of his name because he was content to do things half-way. He did it right, the first time, with no excuses. That's a hard quality to find anymore.

Discipline and respect

When I think back about when I grew up, one thing that strikes me as different then from today is the lack of discipline and respect that parents expect of their children nowadays. When I was young, my parents demanded respect from all of us. As kids they made us do things right the first time, and they did not accept excuses. If right was white and wrong was black, there was a plain line between the two, and there wasn't any talking your way out of things, either. You knew you were wrong when you did it, and your parents knew that you knew you were wrong when you did it. Wrong is wrong. The problem today is that people start to compromise what they think is white and black, and that's where all this gray area comes from. I'm telling you that there's no such thing as a gray area. There's only white and black. I've heard a teacher tell my grandson that if you take something that's less than a dollar it's not really stealing. Now that's just crazy, but these are the kinds of things that society is teaching our children now.

The only time that I ever got a spanking from my dad when I was a child was when I did something that I knew was wrong; I played on a haystack. Haystacks took a lot of work to build, and if that hay was disturbed, the next time it rained the whole pile would be ruined. Without hay, you can't feed your livestock, and all of us kids knew that the number-one rule was never, never ruin a haystack. Well, my sister Rosemary and I did just that, and I'll never forget what happened next.

My dad was in an orchard way up on the hill, and when he came out of those trees and saw the two of us making that mess, he let out a holler and started down that hill as fast as he could come, running down the hill and breaking off a switch from an apple tree at the same time.

I looked up at him and hit the ground running. "He's not using that limb on me," I thought and took off over that cow

16

pasture. "That old man can't catch me." I don't know where I thought I was running to, but I was nine years old and I'd figure it out when I got there. About that time the palm of his hand hit me right between my shoulder blades and I started plowing that cow pasture with my nose. My dad jerked me up by my collar and put marks on my legs with that limb that I know were on there for better than two weeks. Believe me, I never gave him the opportunity to use a switch on my rear end again. He did it right the first time, and he never had to remind me of that again.

My kids come to me today and tell me that they have a problem disciplining their children, and the only advice I can give them is that they need to explain the difference between right and wrong to their children. I tell them that if they spank them one time, and do it right, that they will never have to spank them again, because they're not going to forget it. Now, you can't abuse your kid, but you can spank a child without abusing him. If you spank him good enough, he won't cross that line again. If the teachers in schools today could spank a student, it would probably happen when he was in about the second or third grade, and if he was disciplined right that one time, the rest of the time he was in school he'd never cross the line again. That's the problem today: there's just not enough discipline.

Early education

I was six years old when my dad first started taking me to the old Louisville Haymarket, and that was a real experience. Back then, all the grocery stores were independently owned, and they would purchase their produce directly from the farmer. So, about five in the evening, we'd pack up the truck and head for the Haymarket so that we could start selling our fruits and vegetables that evening and early the next morning. That's when my dad gave me my first lesson in marketing: how to create your own supply and demand.

The first thing my father made sure that I understood was that you had to be honest in all your dealings. Without your credibility and integrity, it's virtually impossible to sell anything to the same person twice. If a grocer asked my dad what kind of apples he had, and my dad said they were good, then that grocer knew that my father wasn't lying to him. I saw a lot of farmers cover their poor quality produce with their very best, to try to fool buyers into thinking that the whole bushel was good. Trying to get a person to buy from him again after he's found out that he's been cheated is just a waste of time. That's why we always did pretty well for ourselves at the market, because people knew that they could trust us. After people know that you're a man of your word, they'll do all kinds of business with you.

My father also taught me that it's just as easy for you to cut your own throat in business as it is for somebody else to. Take apples, for example. If there were five grocers, he would divide all his apples among the five of them. If he had twenty bushels, and one store wanted ten of them, he'd say, "I'm sorry, but I just won't have enough for everybody else if I give you ten, but if you take five today, I can get you fifteen tomorrow." Of course, he told the guy down the street the same thing, and there's no telling how many bushels he had sitting at home, but he wasn't about to flood his own market. He'd meet their demands, and create his own supply. That way, the value of his produce would stay high, and he could sell more apples over a longer period of time.

The same thing is true today. If the labor market is full of people wanting to work, then the cost of labor is low, but if you can find a place where the demand for your skills is high, and the supply of people who can perform that task is low, then your value just shot through the roof. That's why college kids today have such a hard time finding jobs after they graduate: either they don't have the skills that people want, or they're trying to get into a field that's already saturated. With a little more thought or effort, every one of the college graduates today could have a job.

It wasn't enough for us to learn our lessons only in the Haymarket, though; my mother also pushed us at home. She constantly preached on how important it was to have good grades and a good education. My mother loved reading books of all kinds and encouraged her eleven children to do the same to broaden our minds. I heard my mother tell me this a hundred times, and I heard her tell my brothers and sisters a thousand: "Stand up straight, put your shoulders back, and learn to E-NUN-CI-ATE!" and she'd almost bite those syllables off every time she said them. She was really a stickler about how you talked and presented yourself to people, and most importantly, she really pushed us to excel in school.

My Grandpa Koetter was the same way. He lived with us the last seven years of his life, and whenever we finished supper, he told us boys to stay put, that we were going to have arithmetic. He taught me my multiplication tables to twenty-four. The schools only required you to learn to twelve, but that wasn't good enough for him. He'd spew out arithmetic problems and make us sit there and figure them out in our heads, wouldn't even let us use pencil and paper. "If you took thirty bushels of cantaloupes to the market, and you sold them for two dollars and sixty cents, how much is that?" Then, while we were trying to figure that up he'd look us right in the eyes and tap his cane on the table just to try to make us lose our concentration. He gave us problems for an hour every night, and I can figure in my head better than kids today can with a calculator, and I can beat them. Just like my dad, Grandpa taught us to think before we did something. Think!

My dad, on the other hand, had a different way to make us exercise our minds. He taught us to play pinochle. "Watch the tricks! Think about what you're playing! Think!" More importantly, he conditioned us to be competitive and win. Around that table we were expected to go at it as hard as we could to try to win, and there was no cheating. It never even crossed anybody's mind. There never has been any excuse for dishonesty. My dad taught us to play pinochle the same way he taught us to go through life: competitively, honestly, and to the best of our ability.

One thing I've learned over the years is that honesty is never punished. I remember the nuns back in grade school: strict disciplinarians, well educated, honest women. If you got out of line they wouldn't hesitate to crack a ruler over your knuckles. Well, I only got one spanking in elementary school from one of these nuns, and for about forty years I thought it was because I had told the truth. The whole story is that we were practicing for a school play after Mass one Sunday, and we were all supposed to be carrying a "pretend" candle across the stage. All of us boys started to blow out those "pretend" candles as hard as we could. Well, that just made that nun so mad. "You're in the house of God making all that racket! Who did it?" We all did it! We were only kids, but I was the only one who admitted it, and I got a spanking for it. All my life I thought I had been spanked for telling the truth.

I went back to see that nun after she retired. I guess I was

19

forty-some years old. I said, "You know, you were the only nun who ever gave me a spanking when I was in school, and I got a spanking because I told the truth." Now she was an old lady by this time — imagine all the children she had taught — but she remembered what I was talking about without my ever reminding her about it, and replied, "No you didn't, you got spanked because you were acting like you blew out that candle!" It took me forty years to figure that out.

High school

When I got into high school, I had two teachers that I'll never forget. The first was Merle Trainor. He was my physics teacher, and of course we had a real good relationship with each other because he was an excellent mathematician, and Grandpa Koetter had taught me to figure in my head faster than the other students in this class could on paper. He affected me because he pushed us to use every ounce of our energy in his class. He reinforced what my family had always taught me: "You can do it, you can do it, you can do it."

The other teacher was Claude Craig, and he was my Vocational Agriculture and Animal Husbandry teacher for four years in high school. Now, my father had a sixth-grade education, and his way of keeping the books of the farm was through his checkbook; but the first thing Mr. Craig taught me when I was a freshman was how to keep the books for my father's farm. He taught us about farm maintenance, animal care, soil texture, all that stuff, and he was tough. He really taught me a lot of what I know today about farming.

One day during class, a bunch of guys got to passing around a picture of a naked girl, sneaking it around from desk to desk. Well, he caught them. "Bring it up!" he hollered. They took it up, and he took one look at it, turned around and tacked it up to the bulletin board. "There," he said, "now we can all see it and get back to class." That picture stayed up on his bulletin board for over a week, and that was a change of pace back in 1949. It was also the first naked girl that I'd ever seen.

Aside from that, we had a great relationship outside of school because I loved agriculture and so did he. He couldn't afford his own farm because he was a teacher, but every Saturday he'd come up to ours and drive around on the tractors and play with the animals just like a big kid. Farming was his true love, and his enthusiasm for it wore off on me.

Those two men helped make the bulk of my high school experience quite pleasant, but it started out anything *but* pleasant. I was born and raised in a Catholic community, and everybody I knew was Catholic. Borden, where I went to high school, was Protestant. The animosity that was between those communities you wouldn't believe. I mean, it was crazy. We didn't talk to people from Borden, and they didn't talk to us. It was a pitiful shame. You dealt with them every day in business, but you could not be social friends; and for a Catholic boy to go to school with them was tough. They just weren't going to accept me. I didn't have a problem with their being Protestant, but they sure had a problem with me, because I was one of the first Catholics ever to go to school in Borden.

The teachers always treated me fine, but the problems came from the community. I never will forget, in September of my sophomore year, we were down on the softball field. The softball team was having practice, I was catching, and there was a fellow on third base. This guy had been in all kinds of trouble; he was kind of a bad egg. Well, the batter hit the ball, and this guy started barreling down the third base line. When he got about thirty feet from me he said, "I'll tell you one thing you 'so-and-so' Catholic. I'm gonna knock you on your 'rear.'" They winged that ball into me, and I caught it and tagged him out; of course, he hit me like a ton of bricks and after a good roll in the dirt he came up swinging. I tell you what, we had the worst fight that you've ever seen. After they broke it up, we went down to the principal's office and we got expelled from school for three days.

When I got home, I couldn't tell my mother, so I went outside to tell my dad that I'd gotten expelled from school for fighting. He asked what the fight was about, and I told him. He told me not to worry about it, that everything was going to be all right. About 8:30 that night, there was a knock at the door, and it was the principal from the high school. He told my dad, "I need to talk to you and Junior." He asked, "Why didn't you tell me what the fight was about? We would've never condoned that!" I told him that things never were any different than they were down on that ball field, except that this time we kind of fought over it. He looked at me and my dad and said, "Well, that's not the way I run school, so you come on back to school in the morning, and you'll never hear anything about this again." From that day on, I never heard anything else about my being Catholic, and I'm sure that the principal had a lot to do with that; but I think it ended because I had finally stood up to someone. After that, I was elected president of the class for three straight years and had the lead role in all of our class plays. That one fight had broken it up for the whole community.

Uncle Edward Koetter's community spirit

Edward was Grandpa Koetter's oldest son, and he took over the farm when Grandpa passed away. When electricity came through here in 1941, Uncle Edward was the one who went through Starlight and got people to sign up to be in the R.E.M.C., Rural Electric Membership Cooperative. Our getting electricity would be based on whether we could all cooperate with each other, and Uncle Edward was the one who made it happen. He was a very "cooperative-minded" person.

When the electricity started coming through here, somebody had to wire the houses, so he and one of his neighbors took six weeks of schooling on how to wire houses and barns, and they wired every house here in Starlight. They probably charged about fifty cents an hour for their time, but he was more concerned with the importance of getting electricity. Electricity meant prosperity. With better production, there came more money, with which you could buy better trucks; and with new trucks, you could sell your goods to more places than just Louisville. Edward knew how important it was for this community to work together.

I give speeches around the country, and I've seen it happen more than once that an agricultural community shoots themselves in the foot because they couldn't work together. Champagne, Illinois, was the largest producer of strawberries in the country, but none of the farmers up there could figure out that, if they kept undercutting each other, before long they'd all be out of business. That community is all but dried up now. That's not how it works here in Starlight, though. We all work together as a team. If I can't give somebody a good product, I send them down to Stumler's Orchard or my cousin's winery, and they do the same for me. That customer will go home satisfied, and he'll come back; but if we just sent him back home, he'd never come back to Starlight again, and pretty soon this whole community would be gone. Uncle Edward is the one that instilled that cooperative community spirit that you'll find up here between all the farmers.

"Quality is job one"

In the fall of 1952, when I was nineteen years old, my brother Charlie and I went to work for the Ford Motor Company. We went over there to apply for a job, and six hundred people were in line trying to get a job. Ford was then, and still is today, a good place to work. If you had a job at Ford, you were doing something. Our interview went like this:

"What do you guys do?"

"Nothing."

"Well, what have you been doing?"

"Working on a farm."

"What experience do you have?"

"None."

"What kind of farm do you have?"

"Raise fruits and vegetables. Pick stuff, haul it to market. Milk cows . . ."

Finally, he asked, "Well, do you know how to work?"

My brother Charlie said, "We work harder than anybody in here."

The only other two questions he asked us were, "Can you pass a physical?" and "When can you start?" Out of six hundred people, Charlie and I got hired right on the spot, because they knew what country boys were about.

Everybody should work an assembly line for six months. I was nineteen years old, and everything they asked me to do, I did it. That's all I knew to do. If my dad asked me to do something, I did it. So the first thing I did was put six bolts in above the radiator. That was my whole job. Make sure those bolts were in. Then after I got good at that, they asked me to start connecting all the lamps to the wiring block, too. I did it and went on. Then, they said, "Why don't you go ahead and put the hubcaps on one side of the car?" The next day they took that hubcap job away from me and gave me another wiring block. The next day they told me to start hooking up the taillights also. Then the next day they came and gave me the hubcap job back.

We ran thirty-six cars through there an hour, and worked ten-hour days. In one day, I'd jump down from that line onto a hard concrete floor three hundred and sixty times. My legs started hurting me so bad I thought I was going to die. I'd do all those jobs in one minute and thirty six seconds, all the time at a dead run. Nobody around me was working like I was. One day I asked my supervisor for a little rubber mat to put over that concrete to cushion my jumps and he told me that if I couldn't do my job to quit. He went on to remind me that there were six hundred guys outside that wanted my job.

March came, and I was so worn out I guess I had an attitude on me that was unreal. My dad finally told me that I didn't realize what I was doing to everybody. He told me that I was snapping at every person who said something to me, and if I was going to keep that job, I was going to have to move out. However, he said, if I quit that job, I could come back and work for him.

The next morning I tried to get ahold of my supervisor before work started, but I couldn't, so I decided to work until he got there. He finally came in and as soon as I saw him I jumped off that line and said, "Mr. Warren" — I'll never forget his name — "Mr. Warren, I quit."

He said, "You can't quit," and I said, "I have asked and asked you to help me out here with just a piece of rubber, and you won't even do that for me. I've done a good job for you, I've worked hard, now I'm quitting, and I'm going to sit over there on that box for the rest of the day and watch you get three men to try to do what I've been doing. What's more, you're going to pay me to sit there." He told me to go punch out, and I replied, "Ain't no way I'm punching out and if you touch my card I'm going to whip your . . . 'tail.'" For the rest of the day I sat there and watched three relief men bumble around and try to do my job. At the end of the day, I got up, punched out and started walking toward the door, when here he came. He caught up with me, handed me a box of King Edward cigars, and said, "You were right. My job is to get all the work out of a man that I can get, and I have never had a man work like you. You're right in quitting; I'd end up killing you because you haven't got the sense to say no!" So, he patted me on the back, and I walked out the door and went back to run the farm for my dad.

Raging bull

My dad's health had been deteriorating for some time. You see, in 1941 we had a big, black jersey bull. This was a fifteen-to sixteen-hundred pound bull, and he had a mean streak in him a mile wide. In order to control that bull, we had put a ring that was about three inches in diameter through his nose. A chain ran through the ring, which was long enough to trail back between his legs, so that if he started to charge, he would step on the chain and it would pull his nose down and stop him right there.

One evening in August of that year, my dad decided that he would cut through the pasture so that he could drive the cows in on his way home. As soon as he walked into the pasture, that bull jerked his head up in the air, snorted, and came after my dad; he had broken the chain. When he charged, my dad put his hand up and started to back away, and yelled as loud as he could to my brother Paul, who was nearby, "Bring the shotgun!" As long as he was backing up, he was OK, but he stumbled on a clump of orchard grass and went down.

As soon as he fell, that bull was on top of him. This monster got his feet up on my dad's chest and broke every rib in his body; burst his lung; ruptured his spleen; ruptured his liver; cut up his face; tore his ears. It was horrible. It was a miracle he ever got out of that pasture, but my dad grabbed that ring in the bull's nose and twisted it as hard as he could, and eventually that hurt the bull so bad that he backed away just far enough for my dad to roll under the fence. My dad got up, took the shotgun from my brother and fired a shot into the bull's shoulder. Then he climbed back over the fence, chased the bull down to the barn, and shot him again when he started to charge one more time.

When my dad started walking up to the house, all I could see was blood. They rushed him to the hospital, and for six days he was in bad shape. After that, he started to get a little better. He was in the hospital about three weeks, but from that day on, my dad's health was never the same. As it turned out, he developed emphysema from having his lungs hurt so bad. In any case, fourteen men from around the community loaded that bull, which by this time had gone completely mad, into a truck and took him off the old Bourbon Stockyards, where they were paid ninety-nine dollars for him. My dad's hospital bill for that three-week stay was one hundred and two dollars.

Recipe:
Beef Noodle Soup

water   4 carrots
1/2 gal. tomato juice   5 stalks celery
5 to 8 lean beef short ribs   1/2 tsp. celery seed
1 onion   salt and pepper to taste

                                  Noodles
6 eggs   6 tbsp. water
flour

Chop vegetables. Place with meat, water, and tomato juice in an 8 to 10 quart kettle. Simmer two hours. Meanwhile, mix eggs and water and add flour until you get a dough you can roll out on a cutting board. Slice into 1/4-inch strips, add to soup and simmer one more hour.

Bonnie Kruer and Joe Huber, 1949.

3

Bonnie and Joe

Ever since the second grade, I knew who the special person was going to be in my life. I met Bonnie Kruer when I was in grade school. Bonnie was raised on a large dairy farm about a mile and a half from our farm, and on the weekends, Bonnie's family would let her come to our farm and pick strawberries to make a little extra money. So Bonnie began picking at the young age of six and has continued all her life. Back then, I really didn't know what a "girlfriend" was, but I knew that Bonnie Kruer was going to be my girlfriend forever. However, it took me a heck of a long time to convince her that I was going to be her boyfriend, let me tell you!

Bonnie was one of those girls that was really popular at our school. There were plenty of other girls that I could have gone after, but Bonnie was the girl that I wanted. I did everything I could to spend time with her. The nuns at St. John were very strict and they didn't want us talking during school, so I had to find another way to tell her my feelings. Besides, when a boy talked to a girl, the other boys would tease him because they thought having a girlfriend was funny at that age. So that's when I decided I would start writing Bonnie notes. I wrote her notes, usually one per week, for the remainder of my grade school years. Bonnie and I really didn't start our real relationship until about the seventh grade when we shared our first kiss on the playground at school. After that we knew we had something very special that was going to last a long time.

Bonnie didn't get to go to high school because her father didn't believe in it, so she had to stay at home while I went to high school in Borden. This could have put our relationship in trouble if we had not been as committed as we were. Fortunately, one of Bonnie's sisters was the school bus driver and I would talk to her about how Bonnie was doing. Each day as I was going to school I would give Bonnie's sister a note to take to her. Then the next morning her sister would bring me a note from Bonnie. In my four years of high school there was never a day that Bonnie and I didn't have a note for each other. Also, Bonnie worked at a shirt company in town, and I would go and see her every day during my lunch at school. We did all of these things just so we could talk to each other on a daily basis. Now, that's what I considered being totally committed!

Early dating experiences

About the time that Bonnie and I were fifteen years old there happened to be a priest named Father Marcellus Fisher who was really involved with the youth at our church. Father Marcellus would go on dates to the drive-in with Bonnie, me, my cousin, and Bonnie's sister, both of whom were interested in going to the convent. Father Marcellus was somewhat of a character, especially to those girls! At the drive-in he would wait till those two girls had to go to the restroom, then he'd move the car so that they couldn't find us. Father Marcellus would do this all night long, just laughing and having a great time. We were lucky to have someone that took a real interest in the youth of the church and who was committed to helping us when there was something we needed. I sometimes think that people don't use the resources of the church today to help their children to grow and develop. They could be missing out on people who really care about the youth of today, like Father Marcellus did for us.

At our church we had our Catholic Youth Organization, which I was very active in, always being a youth officer. In those days, it was really hard to get people around for youth activities because we were limited to one car per household. So, we were very fortunate to have my dad's ton-and-a-half truck that we could use to go to Clifty Falls State Park in Madison. You see, Madison was the place to go because they had a really nice public pool and we'd go swimming during the day and then spend time running around Madison in the evening. This was a real treat to us because it was a chance for us to get away and still be around people that believed in doing the right things. In addition to our trips to Madison, the Catholic Youth Organization would hold dances throughout the communities, which gave us lots of opportunities to meet other church-going kids outside of school and away from Starlight. This provided us with a good network of friends that we could depend on if we had any problems or needed help.

In those days, it was highly unusual to be on a date by yourselves. You must understand that our families had only one car and there was a lot of competition to use it, especially on weekends! I was lucky, though, because my sisters went to high school at the Academy in Ferdinand, which is about seventy miles west of Starlight. My sisters were allowed to leave school on Friday and I was the one who would go and pick them up on the weekends and then return them to school on Sunday afternoon. When my sisters graduated from high school they went to St. Joe's Hospital in Louisville to go to nursing school. They boarded at St. Joe's while they were there, and again, I'd go pick them up on the weekends. Bonnie didn't mind riding along with me to pick them up and return them, since it was a chance for her to get out, too. Just hustling my sisters back and forth gave Bonnie and me a lot of time to spend together.

I learned a lot during this time about how to share things in life. Donnie Huber, who was my cousin living at the Winery, and I would often go on double dates together, which is kind of funny because Bonnie at one time really had a crush on Donnie. Anyhow, Donnie and I were very close and we considered ourselves like brothers. We both were at the age where we wanted to be able to go out on dates in the car, so what we would do is take turns driving our parents' cars. If I couldn't get the car then Donnie would try, and if he couldn't then I would try. We both realized that our brothers needed the cars to go out, too, so we really had to plan out our dates ahead of time. It was just a matter of communicating to our brothers in advance if something special was coming up. Being in such a large family, I learned the importance of communication and negotiation when it came to planning things, which I believe has really benefited Bonnie and me. This lesson I learned as a youth has been one that I continue to use and have passed on to our children.

Stuck out in the snow

Bonnie and I did have the chance to go out by ourselves

every once in awhile. The thing we really enjoyed doing was going to the Grand Theater in New Albany, where it only cost fifty cents to see a movie. Then after the movie, we went to a local drive-in restaurant where we would order through a speaker and they would bring the food out to the car. These dates were very inexpensive, only costing about three dollars for the two of us. This was our regular date when we were courting in high school.

Now, Bonnie's dad was a very strict man when it came to Bonnie's curfew. Her curfew was 12 midnight, no later and no exceptions! Bonnie's father raised eleven children and each child had the same 12 o'clock curfew. One night, Bonnie and I were in the Grand Theater watching a movie. When we came out we saw that it had been snowing like a son of a gun, and we'd had no idea that it was even supposed to snow! I told Bonnie that we had better head straight to Starlight; there would be no time for cheeseburgers tonight. On the way home it was really slick, and there was about six inches of snow on the ground. We got stuck on a hill, so I turned the car around looking for another road to Starlight. Now, no matter which way you come to Starlight you've got to go up a hill, so I knew that I was going to have to get moving fast to make it to the top of one of the hilly roads. All around the area, there were cars backed up because people were stuck trying to get up the hills. Finally, I found a hill that was clear, so I fired up that black 1947 Plymouth and headed up. I got about two thirds of the way to the top, when I realized we were stuck. Fortunately, my friend Ed Kirchgessner came along behind us and he had some chains that we could put on his car's tires. I said to Ed, " Let me help you put on those chains and you can push us up the hill." We jacked up his car, put on the chains, and he pushed us up and over the hill. We finally got to Starlight and were about a quarter of a mile from Bonnie's house. That house was lit up as bright as can be because the entire family had been waiting for Bonnie and me, since it was 12:20 and we were definitely late. We pulled in and her dad was waiting for us, wearing his bib overalls with one strap hanging down. Bonnie's father was Dutch and he used the expression "By Jingles" when he got really angry. Now, I had heard him say that a lot of times, but he had never said it to me. As we came in the door he said, "By Jingles, vere you veen?" I told him that we were inside the movie theater and when we came out there was snow covering the ground. I told him that we headed straight home and got stuck on one of the hills on the way, which caused us to take two hours instead of a half hour to get home. I explained to him that was the only reason why we were late and that we would't have been if it wasn't for the snow. He exclaimed, "You mean to tell me that you ain't got enough sense to walk outside to see if it was snowing?" There were no excuses for him, and that was the only time Bonnie's father ever raised his voice to me. From that time on, her dad and I developed a pretty good relationship, and he really stood up for me a couple of times down the road.

Second thought and doubts

I can honestly say that Bonnie and I never really had any serious arguments while we were dating, but we sure had some "differences of opinion." When Bonnie was around the age of nineteen she had a sister that was in the convent. Bonnie believed that maybe she should go to the convent to see if becoming a nun was her calling for life. Now, this was definitely not in my "game plan" for Bonnie to go and become a nun while I stayed in Starlight without her. So we had some serious conversations about this desire to become a nun. Fortunately, she didn't become a nun, because I believe I would have had a fit without her as my wife. At no time during our relationship did we ever decide to break up, though. We were very committed to one another and we knew we had a strong bond.

In 1950 Bonnie's sisters tried to get her to go on a date with another boy. Now, Bonnie and I were going steady and we didn't date other people. That was the way we always wanted it to be! Her sisters believed that Bonnie had been missing out on some chances to meet and date somebody new, so they were discussing her dating some new guy. Now, her dad was there at the kitchen table while her sisters were trying to convince Bonnie that she should date someone else for a while. He listened to the entire conversation and finally he blurted out, "By Jingles, vhat I vant to know is vhat the hell is the matter with Joe Huver." After he said that, the conversation ceased and her sisters never brought up Bonnie dating someone else again. That night when I came to pick up Bonnie for our date, her father told me, "By Jingles, I straightened these people up about jou," and that to me was assurance that her father gave his blessing with regard to my marrying Bonnie. You see, Bonnie's father passed away before Bonnie and I could marry and I never really had a chance to ask him for his blessings upon our marriage, but I will never forget how he stood up for me to Bonnie's sisters in 1950.

I also remember something that really got her mother's respect at this time. When Bonnie's father passed away, I was going to be there for Bonnie, and I decided that I would take her to her father's funeral. Her mother really respected the fact that I cared enough to really support Bonnie and her family when such a traumatic event had occurred.

The big question

Bonnie and I dated for a long time and I believe that she thought that we were never going to get married. However, I made the decision to ask Bonnie to marry me in 1953. I told Bonnie's mother of my decision and she supported me one hundred percent. I went to a local jewelry store and I bought Bonnie an engagement ring. I wanted to ask Bonnie to marry me on August 5, which is her birthday. It wasn't dark when we drove over to Shawnee Park to a spot that overlooked the Ohio River, but night fell upon us quickly. Bonnie asked me what I had gotten her for her birthday and I responded that I had gotten her a real nice radio with a record player. I told her that I had ordered it and that it wasn't going to be ready for delivery for some time. Now, Bonnie was so disappointed because she really wanted that record player, but she knew that I had something to give to her that night. So, I opened the glove compartment and there was the ring box with the ring inside. I gave her the ring and asked her to marry me. Bonnie cried a little bit with her excitement and I could tell she was happy, but the first thing that she said was, "I want to go home to see Mom." So that's what I did: I took her home to her mother so she could tell her about our engagement.

My family had no problem with my engagement with Bonnie, probably because our families grew up together. When I asked some of my relatives what they thought of Bonnie they said they were very happy with my decision. My brother Paul felt that he really had something to do with bringing Bonnie and me together because of all the teasing he did about our relationship. This teasing was something of a tradition, which started when I was around ten years old and my mother got me some Superman pajamas. My brothers and sisters would always laugh at these pajamas and ask me, "Joe, are you going to fly out in the middle of the night to go and see Bonnie Kruer?" I believe if I could have flown out to see Bonnie I would have every night, because she was the only girl and continues to be the only girl for me.

Values of those days compared to today

If you wonder whether I ever thought about having sex before I was married, well, let me tell you, I never considered sex until, and only until, I married the woman that I love. In Starlight, when I was growing up, everyone knew each other. If someone were to get pregnant it was a big scandal. It would put shame on the family and they would have to explain to other neighbors about what happened for years to come. Now, this didn't happen very often around here because there was so much family pride. As you know by now, my family had a great amount of family pride and I didn't want to shame the Huber name. The family in those days was not just your mother and father; it was your grandparents, aunts, uncles, and everybody that had any connection with your family. Therefore, I had morals and values that came from everybody I saw on a daily basis. My grandfather would watch me like a hawk when I was in church or praying the rosary to make sure I wasn't playing around when it came to something as serious as church and God. With all these people having so much influence on my life I knew that I couldn't cause them any shame. So, I put sex out of my mind. My mother always would say, "Joe, when you are in this house, your father and I can control what you do, but when you walk out this door you are responsible for your own actions, and remember that you are a Huber!" I was always taught to do what was right because that was the only way to live. This really put pressure on me not to engage in premarital sex, because we were told this was wrong and we had to do what was right!

When it came to talking about sex, when I was younger, I didn't learn from my parents; I learned about sex from talking to my older brothers and their friends. Also, Father Marcellus, the local priest, took a very active role in my sex education. I remember him talking to me about sex and why it was important that I didn't think about it till I was married. He strongly emphasized the importance of being a virgin at your wedding,

35

and that your wife-to-be was to wear a white wedding gown as a symbol of purity. He wasn't the only person that influenced me not to have sex before marriage. When I was in school at Borden my vocational agriculture teacher always told me if I wanted to stay out of trouble then I shouldn't have sex. He would say, "What the hell do you think you are going to be able to do in life when you have to support a wife and child at the age of sixteen." He really put fear in me to keep me from trying to have sex before I was married. I believe that these people influenced me, along with our Huber family pride, to wait till I was married before having sex.

Now, before Bonnie and I were married we were to go and see the parish priest once a week for six months discussing issues that were important in a marriage. Father Marcellus would give us books that talked about sex in great detail. He would ask that we read the books together saying, "These books are going to arouse you, but when you feel aroused I want you to close them and go home." There were many nights that I felt I could break down because the temptation was so immense, but I was committed to waiting.

In today's society I don't think that we demand the discipline or responsibility that I had placed on me when I was a child. My parents expected me to be the best in school and be the top of the class. My mother would ask me all the time, "Did anybody beat you on that grade, who beat you, and how much did they beat you by?" In my twelve years in school I only had one C because of the discipline and the commitment to pleasing my family. I was so scared to take that report card home and show my parents; I knew they would be disappointed because a C was not acceptable. The type of demand that I had from my parents in those days is definitely not present in today's families. Now, I'm sure there are some exceptions, but they are few and far between. This type of demanding of respect and responsibility, and the discipline that was instilled in me really helped me when it came to making many of the decisions in my life. One of the greatest decisions that I made was to carry on these family traditions that were given to me when it came to the importance of doing the best thing and being totally committed to the family. I hope you learn from this and carry it on to your family as well.

Recipe:
Pork Roast and Mom's Dressing
Season roast with salt, pepper and seasoning salt. Roast in a 350° oven for 20 minutes per pound or until well done. Pork roast is very good with Mom's dressing (so are turkey and chicken).

2/3 loaf bread, lightly toasted and broken up

2 onions	2 eggs
2 stalks celery	1 tsp. sage
1 apple	1 tsp. salt
vegetable oil	1 tsp. pepper
1-1/2 to 2 cups milk	water

Chop onions, celery, and apple and fry until brown in a little vegetable oil. Add to broken bread. Beat milk and eggs with seasonings. Mix all together, adding water if needed to make it moist enough. Bake at 325° till brown. Serves 8.

The young Huber family around 1970. From left, Chuck, Beverly, Bonnie, Joe III, Joe, Kimmy, and Louie.

4

Before the Farm

B eing raised in a large family in such a small town you really didn't have an opportunity to do many things for yourself. Graduating from high school was quite an accomplishment as I saw it. I set a goal of graduating from high school for myself, not for anyone else, and I really wanted to do something special with my education. I was a very good student, graduated second in my class. A girl, Rosella McKinley, beat me out of being top in my class. When I graduated I think it really opened the door in this community for others to go on to high school and graduate as well. I know it really helped my younger brothers and sisters with their education, because in our family going to high school was not common. Once I was out of school, I made the decision that I wanted to go on to Purdue University and become a veterinarian. I had the chance to go to Purdue on a full scholarship, but as it ended up I never made it to Purdue because of my commitment to my family.

You see, my second oldest brother Charlie was drafted into the United States Army to serve in the Korean War. Now, my dad's health was getting bad at this time, and with all my younger brothers and sisters still on the farm he just needed someone to help on the farm. My father hated "like the devil" the fact that I might not be able to go on to college, but I had a responsibility to my family that I couldn't throw away. This is one of the things that really helped me understand the importance of accepting responsibility for issues of family life. My dad needed my help and I knew that my staying home was part of being a family. I was only eighteen years old and my father made the decision that I was to start managing the farm. This all happened in one day, without any previous notice at all. I walked out onto the back porch that evening with my older brothers and said, "Man, what are we going to do now?" The response they gave was, "Whatever you believe we should do! You know more about this farm than we do, you take more interest in the farm than we do, and there ain't going to be any problems with you running this farm!" That's the way it was ever since I decided to stay in Starlight and skip the opportunity to go to college.

A wedding that I will never forget

Staying here in Starlight was the best thing that could have happened to me because it allowed me to stay with Bonnie. Our engagement didn't last very long. We asked Father Marcellus to perform our wedding ceremony, and I mean to tell you it was a big wedding. We had fourteen people in the wedding party alone! At the wedding, I would say there were close to two hundred people. That was big in those days. Bonnie and I had probably one of the first recorded weddings ever. We recorded our wedding on a 33-1/3 record player that we borrowed from St. Meinrad Abbey. Our wedding was about an hour long, but looking back it sure seemed to go by fast. I can clearly remember how the ceremony went. I remember that one of the special things was having Bonnie's oldest brother sing the Ave Maria in Latin. What a day that was for me, to be marrying the girl of my dreams since the second grade.

After the ceremony, following tradition, we went to Bonnie's home with forty or fifty people to eat a festive dinner. Then that night we had a big wedding dance at the school close to our church. I would say probably two hundred fifty to three hundred people came to the dance. Of course, there was a lot of partying going on because we had beer and everyone was celebrating. A tradition in Starlight is for your friends and brothers and sisters to get ahold of your car, fix it up, and hide it from you. Well, we were not going to let that happen to us. Father Marcellus and I hid my car about a mile and a half from Starlight in a place we thought no one could find. However, I had bought the car from Bonnie's brother Jude, and he had kept an extra set of keys to this car. It didn't take long for our friends to find the car, and Jude moved it to my brother in-law's house and removed the distributor so the car wouldn't run. Bonnie and I had planned to leave the wedding around 11:00

p.m., but when we went to get the car it was gone. Father Marcellus then decided he would assert his authority in the situation by calling the county sheriff.

The sheriff came out to Starlight and told all these friends of ours that they had to go and get the car immediately. While the sheriff continued declaring his authority, one of my cousins from Knoxville took the keys out of his patrol car. There must have been twenty-five to thirty of our friends in a circle listening to the sheriff, as they started pitching his keys around. When he finally realized what was going on, the sheriff started running around the circle like a little kid, making a fool out of himself trying to get his keys back. Finally, the sheriff got so angry they gave him his keys back and decided to tell us where the car was. So we all headed towards my brother-in-law's house to get the car so that Bonnie and I could leave to go on our honeymoon. Well, the sheriff followed us to my brother-in-law's house and got out of his car with his hand close to his gun holster, still very angry. Now, we lived in Clark County and we had crossed the county line into Floyd County, so this sheriff had no jurisdiction. My brother-in-law said to the sheriff, "Gosh darn it, you have no jurisdiction here, and it seems to me that you better change your attitude because re-election is coming up and I don't know if you'll get our votes." Talk about letting the wind out of that sheriff's sails; I mean to tell you, he hastened to apologize and quickly got in his car and let us be. So at 1:00 a.m. we finally got our car and headed off together as newlyweds.

Something that I will never forget is a gift we received for our wedding. Father Marcellus knew that Bonnie had not done much cooking growing up. She never had to cook because her mother always was cooking. So, Father Marcellus gave us the gift of a 144-pack of Mrs. Grass's Noodle Soup so that I wouldn't starve to death. That's something I still remember us laughing about. Fortunately, Bonnie and I lived at her mother's house and her mother continued to do most of the cooking. We had two rooms upstairs in her mother's house that we used as a living room and our bedroom. I want to let you know that we never had any problems living with her mother, and I really enjoyed that time in my life. We didn't have much money, but our being able to live there allowed to me the opportunity to save a little here and there.

41

Starting out on our own

Finally, after about four months, we were able to buy a small twenty-acre farm, right south of the Starlight community, which had a really old house on the land. That house had no running water in it, no bathroom, no furnace, absolutely nothing! We bought it, though, and we proceeded to remodel our home. Bonnie and I worked on this house for about five months, fixing it up so that we would be able to move in. You can't imagine what we did with that place! Now, we had a lot of friends that helped us get settled in and I can remember us jacking that house up so that we could remove the old rock foundation and pour a new concrete one. Not only did we put in a new foundation, we put in oak hardwood floors, removed all the old wallpaper (with plaster stuck to it), put a furnace in, added a room on, dug the septic system for it, put drainage in for the plumbing, and almost died working to get that house livable! Of the twenty acres on this farm only about seven were tillable, with the others being far too hilly, and the first crop we put in was three acres of strawberries. We had decided that this strawberry crop was going to be the way that we paid for the farm.

We didn't have much money because we had put everything into that farm, but something that was really special to me in regard to family was something my uncle Edward did for Bonnie and me. Bonnie really wanted to have an electric stove in the house, but the house was not even wired to handle those types of appliances. I didn't know how to wire an electric stove, so I called Uncle Edward, who knew a lot about wiring, to help. He said, "Sure, just count how much wire you need and I'll pick up the wire and the box." I figured it would take about fourteen feet of wire and I called him back; he said, "I'll come over tonight and we'll get it done." He came down and connected all the wiring up and put the box in the right place. I asked what I owed him for the wire and the work. His response was, "Ah, you don't owe me anything." I told him that I had to give him something so I decided to give him ten dollars. Three days later, it was my birthday. I received a card from him and Aunt Lucille and in that card was the very same ten dollars. That wasn't a typical gift, but that was their way of helping Bonnie and me get started when we needed help.

To add to all that was going on with the house, Bonnie was

eight-and-a-half months pregnant with our first child. We moved into this house on March 1 and Bonnie was due on March 20. We had cut it close getting that house ready so that Bonnie would be able to have our first child in our newly remodeled home. I remember her walking up to the new cabinets that her Uncle Carl put in and not being able to reach the kitchen faucet because she was so pregnant! We didn't know if it was going to be a boy or a girl because we didn't have ultrasounds, but I admit I was hoping to have a boy so that the Huber name would be carried on for certain. March 20 happens to be my birthday, and I remember that morning walking Bonnie all over that twenty-acre farm hoping she would go into labor and our first child would be born the same day I had been. However, it didn't happen that way, and two hours and twelve minutes into the day of March 21 Bonnie had Joe III, the way the Lord must have intended.

Working from dawn to dusk

While I was doing all the work getting that house ready and preparing for our firstborn child, I still had to manage to pay the bills. In 1953 I got a really good job working for the Indiana Gas Company. I was a serviceman, serving all those people who had gas appliances and working all the new connections and the disconnections. I was provided the opportunity to work a lot of overtime, being on call in the evenings and working Saturdays and Sundays so that we could save even more. This money that we were putting away into our savings was for my dream of someday buying my father's farm. So, I worked throughout the day for the gas company, then on the twenty-acre farm we'd bought, and I still managed the farm for my father who was in poor health. We made some good money raising strawberries and canning pickles on that small farm. We did all of our farming without the luxury of owning any of the new farm equipment available in those days. We didn't have a tractor because I couldn't afford to own one, or even a pickup truck! We were strictly a one-car family! I was fortunate that during the thirteen years that I worked at the gas company my brother in-law did too. He would drive one week and I would drive another. Also, much of the time I would be on service watch, which allowed me to drive a service truck to and from home. This gave Bonnie the opportunity to use the car so that she could go out and purchase whatever she might need during the week.

I really enjoyed working for the gas company because it allowed me to get out and meet people. You see, I would have to get into the home of thirty or thirty-five different people every day. Since I was the person going into these people's homes, I was often the only contact they really had with our company. When I walked through those doors into an irate customer's home, they didn't see me as Joe Huber, they saw me as Indiana Gas Company. There would be times I got my butt ripped because of anger built up over bills or service being temporarily out of order. I learned that when I was there they were going to need to blow off steam before I could help them with any of their problems. I realized that until they were done "giving me a piece of their mind" there was no use talking because they were not going to hear me. I believe that my success with this job was because of something that my mother always said to me when I was meeting people: "Stand up straight and present yourself in a good way." Many people have difficulty being in front of large crowds, but I have no problem being in front of a group of four hundred to five hundred people giving them a talk. I believe the experience with the gas company helped me feel more comfortable with people and crowds.

Some people might have felt they were under too much pressure if they had all the things that were going on in my life. I never even considered that I had taken on too much responsibility, not even with the fact that Bonnie and I had four children within a five-year period. You see, I was always taught, through my parents, that you accepted responsibility for all your actions. If you make the decision to be married then you had better accept the responsibility to make that marriage work. Also, as a parent you have a responsibility to your children. This is all part of a commitment to your family that cannot be forgotten. In everything that I did to get my family going in the beginning, I must say that I had no other thoughts except making it work right. It is just that simple to me, that in everything done in life there must be total commitment to family

Emotionally tied to the farm

As I have indicated, I was on the farm working, even when

I was with the gas company. I can remember one particular summer that my brother and sisters, who were still at home, had planted about five acres of cantaloupe. This cantaloupe needed to be picked, hauled to Cincinnati, and sold at the market so that the farm could make enough money. Now, I had two weeks of vacation time saved up, but I didn't go anywhere. I took those two weeks and hauled those cantaloupes for the farm, driving sixteen hours at a time. That was hard work for a vacation, but that meant more to me than taking that time and spending it on something else, because I knew that it was something that absolutely had to be done.

Living on that small farm for five years, raising what crops we could with me working for the gas company, we decided that it was time for bigger and better things. Bonnie and I had worked very hard saving our money and borrowing equipment so that we didn't have to buy anything that we knew we couldn't afford. This patience and hard work allowed us to build a new home in 1959 on my dad's farm. This meant a whole lot to both of us because Bonnie really enjoyed having her very own home built they way she wanted, and for me it was a way to move closer to my dream of owning my father's farm.

Now, it was no coincidence that we decided to build a house closer to the farm. I remember my mother telling my brother Paul, "We have got to do something with this farm because of your father's health. Somebody has got to come back and run this farm so that we can keep it going. I want to get the family together so we can decide what to do about running this farm." At the time there were my two older brothers and myself as the only options to come and run the farm. We came up to the farm, the three of us, to meet with just my mother in the living room. My mother, knowing that my father's health was really bad, didn't want him to hear about the problems with the farm. She was kind of crying, because this was really hard for her to say, but she said, "We just really need one of you boys to make the commitment to run this farm. The girls and Larry and Davie can help with the work, but they need somebody to show them what needs to be done and keep the farm going." My brother Paul said, "Well, I just can't do it with my job, but I can help," and Charlie said, "I won't be able to run it, but I could help also." Paul looked at me and said, "That leaves you, Joe!" I didn't need much time to think about doing it because I had the dream of owning the farm all along. I blurted right out with, "I'll just sell that little twenty-acre farm and build me a house right here close to Mom and Dad so that I can be around all the time."

So that's how we ended up building our house. Every morning I would come down to the farm at 4:00 a.m. and work till it was time for me to go to work for the gas company. I'd come home, take a quick shower, then work a full day. After work I would get home around 5:30, eat a quick dinner, and go back to the farm and work till dark. Bonnie would come with me! She spent countless hours working picking fruits and vegetables with our children to keep my parents' farm going. We worked that farm for the next eight years and we never made a penny. We didn't expect to make any money. That's pretty good commitment to family, I would say! Eight hours of my day were spent working the farm for eight straight years. I spent almost every Saturday and half of each Sunday running fruits and vegetables to the market as well. I was helping my family, helping my daddy, and helping get my younger brothers and sisters through school. In addition, I had to make time to raise four children that we'd had: Joe III, Kimmy, Beverly, and Louie. That took a lot of work and I did it all for the sake of my family. I have worked for family all my life and I'm 62 years old, and I hope that I work for family till the day the good Lord comes and takes me away. The beautiful part about all this was that my wonderful wife Bonnie agreed with it.

My father's last days on the farm

All along, while I was working the farm, my father's health continued to get worse. It got to the point where he couldn't get out of the house by himself. So, I would bring my pickup truck up to the house, get him in, and take him all over the farm. When my father told me, "Junior, you are going to manage this farm on your own," I was scared and must have asked my father's advice one hundred times a day; because he knew, buddy, and I never second-guessed him. My dad was a good farmer, and when I had that responsibility put on my shoulders I found out just how much he did know and how smart he really was about farming. I guarantee you that I never did anything without going to ask my dad first. So, as his health got worse we would drive from this field to that field and I'd show him what we were growing. I can remember going right through the middle of a cantaloupe field running right on top of them just so my father could see. He enjoyed farming so much that it hurt him not to be out in the fields That's why I would drive into the apple orchards and roll the window down — just so he could reach out there to touch the fruit with his hands. Those times I drove out in those fields, I could tell it meant a whole lot to him, because that was his life. My father meant a lot to me and my family, and it was important that I could still make him smile with a simple touch of an apple. I believe that people often take the simple things in life for granted and forget how much they really mean to them. Family and farming sure mean everything to me!

Recipe:

Custard Pie

4 eggs
3/4 cup sugar
1 tsp. cornstarch
1 unbaked pie shell

2 cups milk
1 tsp. vanilla
1/4 tsp. nutmeg

Combine cornstarch with suger, mix into eggs, and add milk and vanilla, stirring until smooth. Pour into pie shell and top with nutmeg. Bake in 450° oven for 10 minutes, then turn oven back to 375° and bake until firm in center.

The Huber family in 1953. Front row, from left, Cecilia, Larry, Mary, Joseph, David, and Carol. Standing, from left, Kathryn, Doris Ann, Norbert, Joe, Paul, Charlie, and Rosemary.

5

Values from My Brothers and Sisters

My mother and father learned wonderful moral qualities and family values from their parents. During their life together raising eleven children, they developed them and passed them on to me, my brothers, and sisters through the example of how they lived their lives. I would like to share with you some examples of how they were passed to my brothers and sisters. You must understand that all these values together have been instilled in all of us, but some of them show in a greater amount in some than in others.

Paul's responsibility

Paul is the oldest in our family, and his being the oldest in such a large family placed a lot of responsibility on him very early in his life. Paul was born in 1927, and as the first of eleven children he was in the position of taking care of the rest of us. You see, Mother and Dad had all eleven of us in a period of twenty years, and mother averaged a new baby every two years. Paul, then, along with being involved with the farming operations from a very early age with my father, was the built-in baby-sitter. He was exposed to many of the daily chores on the farm, as well as taking care of the rest of us. Paul continued to work on the farm till he went into the Marine Corps around the end of World War II. He served our country in the Corps for two years.

When Paul returned from the service, he went to work for Huber Tire Company and worked there several years before he got married. He was always conscious of what my mother and father needed around the farm. I remember that mother was

49

wanting to get some of the modern kitchen appliances that came out after the war. It was Paul who gave mother many of these new appliances because he knew that she couldn't afford them at the time.

Once my father passed away, Paul continued to live up to the responsibility for my brother Norbert and my mother by helping maintain the house they lived in. Also, as my mother's health began to fail, Paul was the person who took charge of making sure she made her doctor appointments on a regular basis and getting her the right medications. The last five months of mother's life, Paul visited her every day and fed her lunch. You talk about a good sense of responsibility, Paul had it; and he was always there to offer good advice for all of us. He was the person that you could go to knowing he would listen and understand your concerns and help you sort out your problems. Paul became a father figure for our entire family; responsibility was a way of life for him and still is today.

Charlie's competitiveness

Charlie was a very competitive man, not very big, but extremely wiry with light-colored hair, blue eyes and freckles. He kind of looked like a picture that would be on the cover of the *Saturday Evening Post,* painted by Norman Rockwell. As a child Charlie had to win every game that we played, no matter if it was just for fun or not.

I never will forget the time that Charlie bailed me out of big trouble. I was in the third or fourth grade and Charlie would have been in around the seventh grade. A boy in the eighth grade had gotten me involved in a game of marbles. Now, I didn't have any marbles and never really knew too much about the game. I played early that morning, at lunchtime, and at recess, and at the end of the day I owed this guy two hundred and seventy eight marbles. He told me that I had to pay up with the marbles the next day or he was going to beat the tar out of me. Boy! I ran home from school and told Charlie about the trouble I had gotten into and how this guy was going to beat the tar out of me if I didn't pay up.

Charlie didn't have any marbles, either, but said "We'll take care of him. I'll make me a marble." We went out to the road bank of the house and found a place that had some orange clay, and Charlie got him some of this clay, molded it into the shape of a marble, and baked it in the wood-burning stove for about three hours. When he took it out it was hard as can be and he painted it with red fingernail polish so that it was the prettiest marble that I had ever seen. The next day we went out to the playground to meet this guy and Charlie said, "I'm going to play you in marbles today and see how bad you can beat me." At the end of the day Charlie won back the two hundred and seventy eight marbles, plus fifty, which he shared twenty five of with me. I learned a good lesson that day: never to get talked into something without thinking it through.

Charlie was very small and I think that had something to do with his competitiveness, because he knew his attitude was needed to make up for his size. I remember that one year we got some boxing gloves and boys twice Charlie's size wanted to box with him. Well, Charlie was a left hander, a very good boxer, and by the end of the match they had realized they had bitten off a little more than they could chew.

Charlie was a big outdoors man and he loved to hunt and fish. He was a super shot, and in the early years, when we hunted quail with our father, nobody could end the day with the number of quail Charlie would have gotten. He was so competitive that he always ended up the winner and he definitely didn't like losing. I remember Paul, Charlie, and I went hunting one day and Paul remarked, "I think by 10 o'clock I'll have my limit," which would have been ten quail at that time. Charlie challenged him by saying, "There will be no singles for you today!" Sure enough, Paul didn't get his limit by 10 o'clock or even by the end of the day.

Charlie took this attitude with him when it came to his business, where he was very successful. He did everything with this competitive spirit. Charlie died at a young age of forty seven, but he got more done in that amount of time than most will accomplish in ninety years.

Norbert's gentleness

My mother had a hard time with Norbert's birth because of his size, eleven pounds and thirteen ounces. Norbert is a little bit cognitively impaired, and mother felt that this was caused by the difficult childbirth she had with him.

Norbert has something that is extremely special to our family in his gentleness. You never will see someone who loves

51

small children the way that Norbert does. They in turn respond to Norbert wonderfully. He loved to be around his nieces and nephews, especially from the time they were small babies till they were around three years old. He loved to pick them up and hold them, coddle them, and make them smile at him. He does the same with his grand nieces and nephews today, as well.

Norbert is a very quiet person and needs his own quiet time, which the farm life here has really given him. Also, it gave him the opportunity to maintain his own independence, and he has done very well working on many of the tasks here that require a lot of patience. Norbert has the patience of Job!

I have had the opportunity to have Norbert here on the farm with me since I purchased it from my mother and father. For twenty-eight years we have spent time together, usually on a daily basis, and the one example that Norbert has always set forth, in his gentle way, is really what our priorities in life should be, the loving, gentle nature that he displays to every-one he comes in contact with. All of my brothers and sisters have experienced his gentleness and he has just been one of God's blessings for our whole family.

Rosemary's sharing

It is important to understand that my mother had three sons before she had her first daughter, Rosemary (Sis); and then I followed. So Rosemary grew up surrounded by boys and she definitely had to have a strong will. Not only did Rosemary have a strong will, she also displayed the value of sharing that my mother and father instilled in us. Rosemary is a Maryknoll nun, and through her ministry as a missionary she has shared her whole life with other people.

Rosemary went to school in Ferdinand at the Academy of the Immaculate Conception and religion was a very important part of her life. While she was there, she was an excellent student and made very good grades. When she graduated from the Academy, she expressed her desire, immediately, to be a Maryknoll missionary. However, my dad encouraged her to wait one year, get a job, and experience life before she decided to become a nun, so she got a job at Huber and Huber Motor Express as a secretary and worked there a little over one year, but she stayed very focused on her desire to be a nun. It was kind of hard for my father to see her go because she was the first daughter, but she left and became a Maryknoll missionary.

Rosemary has a degree in Hospital Administration and she knew this would be helpful for her mission work. Her first assignment was in Korea, where she did her work for about two years before she came back to the United States. Then she and two other Maryknoll missionaries went to Indonesia to help those who needed first aid and other types of health care. It didn't take the Indonesian government very long to find out what her talents were, and they soon had her showing the people in the government how to operate hospitals.

Rosemary remained dedicated to what she was doing, but in some regard she knew that she wasn't fulfilling her need to help the poor and less fortunate. So she requested from her Mother Superior that she be relieved of her duties working with the government hospitals to continue working with the poor on the outer islands. One winter Rosemary wrote us a letter saying how she would like to help the tribe there to purchase some new goats to keep theirs from becoming inbred. So, for Christmas we sent her money to purchase these goats. A little while later, Rosemary sent us a picture of the village chief and the tribe with these newly purchased goats in front of them. I could tell the chief was happy because he was grinning from ear to ear; it was too bad that he was missing four teeth in front.

I will never forget Rosemary telling my father good-bye before she left. They both knew that his time was short and he would probably pass on while she was away, but neither one shed a tear and my father remarked, "I'll see you in heaven." I have no doubt in my mind that will happen some day. Rosemary has a gift of sharing and has continued to share with our family through her letters about her times as a missionary. She comes about every five years and visits with everyone in our family and community, and with the families of other nuns. The value of sharing continues to live on through her actions, and I am grateful.

Doris Ann's perfectionism

My mother and father always expressed the importance of doing things right and this can be observed in Doris Ann (Bitsy) better than in any of the other children. Bitsy had a perfectionist attitude that was unreal. When we were children, we all had the responsiblity of setting the table. Bitsy would be the person who would walk around the table and move every little object on it to make it perfect.

When we were kids working on the farm and packing vegetables to haul to the market in Louisville, Bitsy would be the one that would check all the boxes to make sure that the packing was perfect. Living in Atlanta now, retired from her profession as a registered nurse, Bitsy spends a lot of her time doing needlepoint, and you talk about doing something perfectly, that is exactly the way she does it. She gets top dollar for her work and it is truly an art of the highest quality.

One of the memories I have about Bitsy when we were growing up was around the time I was thirteen to fourteen years old and she was eleven or twelve, about two inches taller than I was, and outweighed me by twenty pounds. Just as most brothers and sisters do, we would horse around and wrestle, and no matter how hard I tried, I could not whip her when it came to wrestling. She sure got a big kick out of being able to whip me since I was her big brother. We still reminisce about when I was a little squirt and she could whip me even though I was her older brother.

Throughout all of her life Bitsy has been a perfectionist. It had to be right or perfect and that was the only way around her. You can see her perfectionism in her home and in her family. Today it is still hard not to have her look over your work and find something that needs to be improved, and that is a value that I'm really glad is in our family.

Kathy's reverence

My mother and father were very religious people, went to church every week, never missed, and took it very seriously. My sister Kathy had a strong feeling about religion and she became a Benedictine nun. She went to the Academy in Ferdinand and through her religious education she made the decision to go directly into the Convent there in Ferdinand and declared her vocation as a nun. She continued her education and received her master's degree in education and taught at many different schools. She served in the role of a Vice Principal and then as a Principal as well. So, not only was she a religious woman, she was an outstanding educator.

To tell you how strong her faith is and how committed she is to her vocation in life at the Convent in Ferdinand, all the members of the monastery elected her as prioress. That is not the only part of it; she was reelected for multiple year terms, which is quite a honor, since there are two hundred and sixty nuns. Kathy really has a challenge to keep all these nuns content and I kidded her when she became prioress by saying, "You are Top Nun, but you are not the Top Gun, and don't you forget it."

Kathy is the type of person who can talk to anyone and is able to comfort them and lift their spirit when they are really down. She has a wonderful talent of being able to deal with people and all of their really deep problems. She always focuses on getting them to be able to look at the bright side of life and to put their lives in the hands of God. Kathy has a saying that all of us need to remember; when she leaves she never will say "Good-bye," she will say, "Be good to yourself." I think that if more people could stop and think about that and start living by that saying we could enjoy life a whole lot more. When we are good to ourselves I truly believe that we are often better to others. Kathy has meant a great deal to our family with her spiritual leadership, and it's pretty easy to know that there is a God when you see the faith that is displayed in my sister Kathy.

Cecilia's spirit

Mother and Dad were always fun people to be around, and when you are around my sister Cecilia you can see the type of fun-loving spirit that has been passed on to our family. We didn't have TV when we were young, but they had soap operas on the radio and one in particular was Ma Perkins, which came on at 12:30 p.m. There was a young lady in that soap opera whose name was Chi Chi and when Cecilia was born the doctor told my father that they had a little girl, and my dad responded, "I've got me a Chi Chi." When she was growing up and people would ask her, "What is your name?" she would reply, "My name is Chi Chi, but my pretty name is Cecilia."

When Chi Chi was born she had a whole lot of dark brown hair, while the rest of the kids were much more blonde. She also had more hair on her head when she was born than most of us guys had when we were two years old, but her hair was beautiful and my mother never cut it till she was around the age of thirteen. I can remember many a morning my mother getting Chi Chi ready to go to school, and it seemed like she would brush her hair for hours.

The spirited type of person she was, she always wanted her hair in braids so she could show it off at school. Whenever I go to the horse races and I see those fillies with their manes braided and acting really fiery, I always think of Chi Chi because she had the spirit of those thoroughbreds. I remember when Chi Chi was at the Academy in Ferdinand and she got into the band and started to play the saxophone. She was a small-framed little girl at that time and I can never forget how big that sax looked compared to her. Well, one afternoon our whole family went to the Academy to see Chi Chi play the sax in a concert. Chi Chi pranced out on the stage and sat in a chair and started playing with so much emotion that her chair looked like it was walking around on that stage. She couldn't play worth darn, but she sure played with some spirit.

When you look at her you can see the spirit inside her and she has that gleam in her eyes that tells you what she is all about — full of spirit — and it can be seen in her children as well. I think that life will always be fun for Chi Chi because she is never afraid to take on a challenge and give it her best.

Carol's kindness

Kindness was always very important to my mother and father; it could be seen in the way they treated neighbors, family, and the community. When we were growing up, Kathy, Chi Chi, and Carol were always referred to as "The Three Little Girls" and still are today. My mother, being a good seamstress, always made the girls new dresses to wear Easter Sunday. She always dressed these three alike, and Carol, knowing that she had nicely made clothes, always seemed to let others girls around the area borrow all of her clothes; it didn't matter if she had anything nice to wear.

I don't think that Carol has ever missed a birthday of any of her five brothers and five sisters over all these years. All these cards she has sent us always have the nicest sayings and always kind thoughts. That is the way Carol is! Carol happens to be a pretty good cook and when she cooks you can always expect that there is going to be plenty so that she can offer everybody something to eat. She comes to visit family around here pretty often and when she does you know she'll always be in the kitchen helping, cooking, and cleaning so that everybody can enjoy.

Carol received her education from the Academy in Ferdinand and then went on to become a public health nurse after attending St. Joe's. She is the director of communicable diseases for the public health department in Marion County, Indiana. She is very dedicated to her job and this is her way to go out and help those who are less fortunate than others. She sees this as her ministry in life, helping other people!

Larry's ethics

I'll never forget the day Larry was born; I was eleven years old, it was May 22, and my brothers Paul, Charlie, Norbert, and I were out in a strawberry field when my dad came out and said, "Guess what, you got a little brother." After four daughters in a row my dad was really excited that he had another son, but the bottom of my world fell out because tradition had it that the youngest was the one who got the farm. I thought to myself, "Oh God, I will never get the farm."

My mother and dad had very high morals and principles in their lives and they told us to be be doers, not talkers. They always were warning us to never talk up a job if we couldn't do it, because the doing of it is the most important thing. You see, my mother and dad were doers by the way they lived their lives, and we learned what morals, principles, and values were all about from watching their actions and listening to their speeches. In my brother Larry, I can really see their lessons in the way he handles life.

Larry worked this farm as hard as any of us did, but we knew that his heart and soul were not in it, and he concentrated highly on academics. He made the decision to go to school over in Louisville at St. Xavier, and that took a lot of commitment. Larry then went on to college at the University of Louisville and took courses at the Speed School, completing his course work with his degree in Civil Engineering. He had a great experience working with the Louisville Water Company and for the state doing a geological study in two co-ops. He became highly qualified working with water systems and was very interested in this field.

He had many interviews after college, and he chose to go to work for a construction company over the Louisville Water Company because the position paid better. He worked for the company for about a year and half, until the president of the

Water Company gave him a call to have lunch with him. Larry said that before lunch the president told him that before he left from lunch Larry was going to be his employee, and that happened to be the way it worked out. Larry started working for the Louisville Water Company and after about two months he told me that someday he was going to be president. Sure enough, twenty-one years later, Larry's dream became reality. I think that this dream came true because Larry showed a great sense of moral values and a commitment to treating people right. Larry is an inspiration to all of our family by the way he gets things done, showing what can be done if you put your mind to it. All of our family appreciates him for his moral strength.

David's consideration

Looking back on David's childhood and how we used to tease him, calling him "Baby Davie," I just wonder if we might have been a bit unfair to him. He always said that our teasing never bothered him, and, David, I hope that it didn't.

For David, being the youngest in the family was probably pretty tough, seeing most of his family moving on as he stayed to work the farm. He worked that farm extremely hard and he really helped my father keep things together. After David graduated from high school at Providence he was kind of confused about what he wanted to do with his life. He decided that he would join the Navy, and he served for four years on the aircraft carrier Intrepid. When David left, I think we all looked at him as still a boy, and I guarantee you one thing, that after he returned home from the Navy, he was a man, a good looking one at that.

The quality of consideration could always be seen in the way that David helped care for my mother and would come to help her in her garden. I never will forget one year that I was planting in the strawberry field and I came across a marijuana plant. I guess it must had gotten there from a bird dropping or something of that nature, so I took it over to show Mother. She knew what it was, even though it was the first time she had even seen a marijuana plant. She said, "Plant it over there in my flower garden. I want to see that thing grow." I responded, "Mother, you don't want that thing in your garden." "Yes, I do!" she said. So, I planted that plant and it was in there for about two weeks until David came out to help Mother with her garden and saw it. He said, "My lands, what on earth are you doing with this plant in your garden? The police are going to catch you and lock you up! I could see it in the paper, 'Mary Huber arrested for growing marijuana.'" So, David took it as his responsibility to get rid of that plant, and he continued to come over and check Mother's garden, just as a way to show her how much he cared.

Not only did he visit Mother, but he visited all his brothers and sisters on a regular basis and you could always expect him to show up at your place. He did this because he really cared for his brothers and sisters and their families as well. He also spent quite a bit of time with our brother Norbert and would always go out on the town with him. They have developed a great relationship, and it is based upon the considerate attitude they have towards each other. David happens to be one of the best friends I have!

These values will continue to be passed down to generations through my brothers and sisters. I want you to know how nice it is to see our mother and dad still living in our lives through the values of today's generations.

Recipe:

Fried Round Steak

Cut meat into small pieces and flour on both sides. Heat oil in skillet. Brown steak on both sides, then let simmer in its own gravy at least a half hour, or until tender.

Corn Bread

2 cups cornmeal	1 tsp. salt
2 cups flour	2 tbsp. butter
1 tbsp. baking powder	milk

Melt butter in pan (a cast iron skillet or corn stick pan works best). Combine dry ingredients and mix with enough milk to make a batter you can pour into the pan. Bake at 425° until golden brown.

Mom's Best Tomato Gravy

6 strips of bacon	1 cup tomato juice
flour	1 qt. water

Fry bacon for grease. Brown enough flour in the grease to make a roux, as if you were making brown gravy. Add tomato juice and water, stirring until smooth and thickened. Serve over cornbread for breakfast. Also good on meatloaf.

The farm today.

6

The Farm

In early November of 1966, my dad called a family meeting so that he could talk to us all about selling the farm. My five brothers were there, but my sisters, because of their professions (three being registered nurses and the other two Catholic nuns) could not make it. Even though they couldn't attend, they made it known that they trusted whatever decision my father made concerning the farm. After we ate dinner, Dad sat at the end of the kitchen table and described for us what he'd like to see done with the farm, and said that he would like for me to have the first opportunity to buy it.

He continued with the way he wanted things to be: how that he thought it would be better if he and I just traded places. He had decided that Bonnie, the kids, and I should move into the farmhouse, and that Mother, my brother Norbert, and he should move into the house that Bonnie and I had just built. When he had finished, he asked all my brothers if they agreed with his decision, and they had no problem at all with anything that my dad had said. Then he made a statement to us that I'll never forget: "If you have any reservations about anything we've talked about, bring it up now, while I'm here, so that we can talk about it, and work it out. I don't want to pass away, and then in a few years have you all arguing about it." It was very important to my dad that family work together; this was his number one priority. The good news is, twenty-nine years later, my brothers and sisters are still the best friends I've got, period!

I believe my dad wanted me to have the farm not only because he knew that farming was my first love, but also because his real concern was for Norbert, my brother. Norbert's a little bit of a slow learner, a little disabled, and my dad was really concerned about what Norbert's lifestyle would be like after he was gone. My dad knew that the farm is something Norbert also enjoys. My dad and I had several conversations where he asked, "Who's going to take care of Norbert when I'm gone? When your mother's gone? What's going to happen to Norbert's life?" I told him not to worry about it, that I would take care of him. Today, everything has worked out the way I think my dad would have wanted it to be.

Family helping family

The decision had been made that I would buy the farm; the only problem left was finding the money. Well, Bonnie and I had some pretty good equity built up in our house, and we had saved all the money I had been paid for overtime hours with the gas company, but it still wasn't enough. So I went to the Federal Land Bank, and they came out and made an appraisal on the farm. They came up with a loan that they could make to Bonnie and me for mortgaging the farm, but it still wasn't enough money. So my mother and dad took the balance of the money we had and sold the farm to me on a contract, and I had the opportunity to pay off that loan over a fifteen-year period. Once again, with my mother and father selling me the farm on contract, and all my brothers and sisters agreeing to the sale, it was family helping family. We all work together.

We didn't end up buying the farm until January of 1967, so I continued to work at the gas company until April 1, because that's when spring breaks and that's when it really gets busy on the farm. It was a tough decision to leave the gas company, because I'd been there thirteen-and-a-half years. I was eligible for three weeks vacation, had hospital insurance and a retirement plan. There was security, and I had the opportunity to work a lot of overtime hours and make some good money, but Bonnie's brother Jude gave me a bit of good advice. I put a lot of faith in Jude and I talked to him about quitting quite a bit, and he said, "I'll tell you what, Joe, you're out here trying to work on the farm. You're trying to work out there at the gas company, and what you build up with your hands here on the farm you're dragging shut with your butt because you can't be here all the time. Quit the job. Come out here and work on the farm, and if it doesn't work out, you can always get another job;

you're only thirty-four years old." So, I quit the job.

It was really tough on Bonnie to see me quit that job, though. I was making good money, and everybody in this community thought I was absolutely crazy to leave it.

A lot of folks would have loved to have that kind of job, but we made the decision that we were going to do it. It was a matter of commitment. I was going to be a farmer and I was going to make it work. That's the kind of commitment it takes.

The tough switch

We moved from a new, modern home into an old farmhouse. There were three little bedrooms upstairs, and there was one larger one down below. The kids were still little at this time — Joe was twelve and Chuck was two, with Kim, Beverly and Louie in-between — and Bonnie was used to living in a ranch house with their bedrooms right outside our door where she could hear them. She was concerned about those children being upstairs where she couldn't listen for them, so she insisted that our bedroom be upstairs with them so that she could be by our kids. In that old farmhouse, though, the furnace only had duct-work heating the downstairs, and being that we moved down there in January . . . well, lets just say that it was very hard for Bonnie to leave her brand new home to move into that old beat-up farmhouse.

But by the same token, it was hard for my mother to leave the old farmhouse to move up to the new one. You have to understand that my mother lived in this home for forty-one years, from 1926 to 1967. This was the home she raised her eleven children in. It wasn't a house, it was a home. There's a lot of difference between the two. After we had moved, I'd go up to Mother and Dad's and Mom would be crying because she missed her old farmhouse. Then I'd go back to the old farmhouse and Bonnie would be crying because she missed her new house. So there wasn't really a place where I could relax for a little bit.

The day we moved into that farmhouse, though, we started to remodel it. Cabinets, the furnace, everything, "Out with the old and in with the new." It wasn't but a little bit until Bonnie was comfortable where she was, and Mom, Dad and Norbert were comfortable in their new home, but it was a pretty tough time for everybody for about four months.

Bonnie is a super, super decorator, and when she got into

65

redecorating that old farmhouse, it really got to be fun because she enjoyed it and she was good at it. What Bonnie has done with that old farmhouse is almost a miracle, and my mother was so proud of it with all the remodeling that Bonnie had done. Every time that somebody would come to see my mother it was always the same thing, "Come down and see the farmhouse." Mother was a built-in tour guide. She enjoyed it because she knew that her old house would be fixed up and taken care of.

Shaping up the farm

My dad understood how to take care of the land. The farmland when I bought it was as good as you could find anyplace. In the forty-one years that my dad worked this farm, he had really built up the fertility of the land. When he bought the farm, he had about fifty-two acres of land that was cleared off; the rest was covered with woods, and he hand cleared those. He sawed down the trees with cross-cut saws and used dynamite to blow the stumps out of the ground. With an ax and grubbing hoe he grubbed the roots out of the ground, and I mean to tell you that's work. This land was in tip-top shape.

The outbuildings were another story, however. The barn and the chicken and hog houses were built back in 1893, so you can imagine how they were starting to look. Now, the house was still in good shape. I remember that my dad had the exterior of the house painted every three years; he repaired the roof and fixed up every little thing whenever it needed it. Also needing to be fixed up was the apple orchard. At that time, it was getting close to forty years old, which is about the life of an apple orchard, and it needed to be replaced. Needless to say, we had our work cut out for us.

So, during that first four months we did a lot of work remodeling the house, but when summer hit, Bonnie and I started farming. We were basically farming just like my dad was, primarily raising cantaloupes, cucumbers, peppers, strawberries, and tomatoes. I took out the old apple orchard and replaced it with five hundred new apple trees that first year, and it was a good feeling just to be working together as a family. My oldest son Joe was twelve, and he already knew how to drive a tractor. (All my boys knew how to drive a tractor by the time they were seven years old.) He would go out and do all the cultivating and discing if it needed to be done, so I got a lot of good help out of him even though he was only twelve.

Why it's worthwhile

Financially, we were all right, but things were pretty tight. We had never spent a whole lot of money even when I was doing well at the gas company. We were always saving so that we could have the opportunity to buy the farm, anyway, so we were used to living fairly simply. One of the big things we used to like to do, though, was go to the drive-in theater, and we went there an awful lot. Bonnie and I would load the kids up: I'd put two lawn chairs in the trunk of the car; Bonnie would pop up a great big plastic bag full of popcorn; we'd take a big Tupperware pitcher full of Kool-Aid and go to the New Albany drive-in. The kids liked to stay in the car and do their own thing, so Bonnie and I would get the lawn chairs out of the trunk and sit outside so that we could have a little peace and quiet with each other. Relaxation at the drive-in. It was a good time, and we did it at least once a week. That's the good thing about working together on the farm; I always have gotten to spend time with my family, and that's worth it all.

My dad passed away in March of 1967, but he knew back in November that his time was going to be awfully short, and that's why he called that family meeting. He wanted to get a lot of this stuff settled before he was gone. It's really hard to give up your parents, but my dad had suffered so badly for the past several years from his emphysema and the injuries that he had from when that big ole bull got him down, and in a way it was a relief to see him get out of all that suffering. My dad and I were really close — all parents are close to their children — and it was hard to lose him, but I can still see him when I look out across the farm, and as long as the farm is here, he will be too.

The winter months

We were farming when it was pretty tough, especially during the winter months when there was no cash flow. When you got past October, you had six months with no money coming in, so the winter of 1967 was really tight. Then in the spring of 1968, the West Clark Community School Corporation decided it was going to add another bus route for its school system, and they put this route up for bids. I figured I could do that for nine months out of the year, six of which were during the really slow months, and it would only take an hour in the morning and one in the afternoon. So I bid on this bus route and I got it. I don't know if I was lucky or not, but the guy bidding next to me was only ten cents more expensive than I was.

I drove that school bus for seven years, and it helped out a bunch. It paid the utility bills, and put groceries on the table through the winter months, but I'll tell you what, driving a school bus was not my thing. I didn't enjoy it, even though it was all right during the winter months, but I hated having to stop working in the afternoons to go drive that bus. I liked the kids, though, and I knew every one of them and their parents. When I first got the bus route, I went around and talked to all the parents and asked them if it was all right with them if I disciplined their children and kept order on my bus. None of them had any problem with that, but that's the kind of people that live in this community. I never had any problems on my bus.

During this time, Bonnie was being a terrific mother with our kids. Bonnie and I really encouraged and worked with our children to excel in school and get good grades. We also encouraged them to be involved with all the sports that were going on at their school, and as a matter of fact I coached our local basketball team for six years. I enjoyed it and it was a way to contribute and give back to the community. But Bonnie and I made the commitment that after our kids finished school up here at St. John's, we would sacrifice whatever we had to to send them to a good Catholic school, and we were able to do that.

Community help

When you farm like we do, growing all kinds of fruits and vegetables, it takes some specialized equipment that you only use once or twice a year. For example, when you raise potatoes, you take a potato planter and use it one day to plant all your potatoes; then when they mature, you a need a potato digger to dig them, and you only need the digger three or four days. We had neighbors in our community that had that kind of equipment and they were happy to let us use it. In the community here in Starlight, people are neighbors, and they help each other. It's been that way since my great-great grandfather was here, and that neighborliness exists even today. If there's

68

a big thundercloud stirring up and your neighbor is out bailing his hay, there's no doubt in your mind what you're going to do. You're going to go fire up your tractor and get all the help you've got and go get that guy's hay bailed. People work together and help each other.

Whenever it gets super busy around here, Bonnie's family is always really good about helping us. Back in those days, Bonnie's brother Jude was what we called a machinery jockey. He would buy used equipment from everywhere, fix it up and sell it. He was also an auctioneer, and he really knew equipment. When I first bought this farm back in 1967, I really needed a tractor that was more modern than anything that was here. Jude had this Ford tractor that I wanted so bad I could die, but I couldn't afford it. He needed to get $4,000 for it, and that was a whole lot of money. I talked to him to try to work out some way that I could pay for it, and Jude said, "My god, Joe, just take the tractor. Go out there this summer and farm, and when the end of the year comes, if you can pay for it, fine. If you can't, just bring the tractor home." Well, how can you beat a deal like that? That's just the kind of family the Kruers are, and that's the kind of help people always gave us.

With that kind of help, it never crossed my mind that we weren't going to make it, but I also was smart enough to know that I didn't know it all. No man is an island, so I really got involved with the Purdue University Indiana Vegetable Growers Association. During the summer, they would have about three "Twilight Meetings" that would start about four in the afternoon on one of the members' farms. The entire staff of Purdue University's agriculture department would attend, and I really learned a lot from them and the other vegetable growers. I also developed some really good friendships within that association. One fellow in particular was a man by the name of Richard Hayden. He could go to another university and talk in all the scientific terms, but he could also come out to your farm and speak to you so that you really understood what he was talking about. He is also a man of really high morals, and he's one of the best friends I've got. This opportunity to be involved with the vegetable growers really helped us to be a better organization. Once again, there was always help there when we needed it. I have never, never been turned down when I asked for help.

Winds of change

All during this time, from 1967 through 1972, we were making some decent money, but I saw, after one year of farming in 1967, that the profit margin was so narrow that there had to be a better way. Bonnie and I kept accurate records, and we got to talking because we knew we were going to have to do something different if we were going to survive on this farm. In our mind, the only way for us to do that as a grower was to sell directly to the consumer. We had to eliminate the wholesale houses that sold to the grocery stores. Those guys were making all the money and we were doing all the work. We could give the consumer a better product for less. It was time for a change.

Recipe:
Strawberry or Red Raspberry Cake

1box white cake mix
1box strawberry or
  red raspberry jello
1/2 cup vegetable oil

1/2 cup water
3/4 cup strawberries or
  red raspberries
4 eggs

Cook berries until hot. Squeeze out juice. Use 1/2 cup cooled juice. Mix dry jello with cake mix. Add oil, water, and berry juice. Beat in 1 egg at a time. Bake in greased and floured loaf or layer pans at 350° for 35 minutes.

Icing
1 box powdered sugar
1/2 stick butter

1/2 cup strawberry or
  red raspberry juice

Prepare juice as above. Combine with other ingredients. If too thin, add more powdered sugar.

The Farm Market.

7

Developing New Ideas

In November of 1967, the Indiana Vegetable Growers Association had a meeting at Purdue University to discuss new ways to be more successful in vegetable farming. This was a small gathering because the association was not large, but these farmers, along with myself, knew a lot about the different ways to grow. We listened to some of the ideas being shared at the meeting, and one man talked about how he opened his field up to his local community so that they could come in and pick asparagus.

After I heard him talk, I realized that it might be possible to do something similar here in Starlight on our farm. This wasn't the first time I had heard of something like this, but it was the first time I had heard of anyone making any real profit. As a matter of fact, in 1966, a year before I bought the farm, I decided to put up a cardboard sign for my father to let the neighbors and those people out for a Sunday drive come in and pick strawberries so that the strawberries wouldn't rot. Bonnie and I got a three-by-three-foot sign and wrote, "Strawberries Pick Your Own." That Sunday we made $44.00 by letting people pick what they wanted. Let me tell you, that was a big deal because that was lots of money at that time.

The U-Pick venture

So, in the spring of 1968 we decided that we would let people come in and pick the strawberries on their own, even before we sent any to market. We had to come up with a way to have a higher profit margin for raising and selling our fruits and vegetables. In order to do that, we had to be able to sell directly to the consumer and eliminate the wholesaler from purchasing and marking up the prices at the grocery stores. The wholesalers were making the money off the fruits and vegetables that we had worked hard to grow and pick and deliver to them. So, we decided to eliminate all these middlemen and sell directly out of our fields at a better price than we were receiving from the wholesaler, and a better price for the customer. Besides, we figured the customer would be more satisfied because they could pick the highest quality products, not get something packaged.

The first time we opened our fields to people it was outrageous. People were coming from all over, ready to pick a whole lot of food. The only problem was they were picking much more than they could handle. These people were picking a hundred and thirty quarts of berries and didn't have any idea how to make jellies or preserves. So we quickly had to put a limit on how many berries we would allow to be picked. Another thing we learned was that we had to start supplying people with containers because they were bringing five-gallon buckets, filling them full, and smashing all the berries on the bottom. We came up with a custom-made box that was only two inches deep so that the berries wouldn't get mashed. There would be no use in our raising a high quality product just to have the customer ruin it by mishandling. Also, we believed it was our responsibility to educate these people on the proper way to pick berries, get them home, and process them so that they would keep. This first year we only tried Pick Your Own with five acres of strawberries, and then we decided to try a half-acre of green beans. Man, was it a success!

The word got out

Now, this success was very limited because we had the problem of advertising, which we definitely couldn't afford at the time. We couldn't go on the radio or TV, so I wondered how we could get the word out to the people that we were in business. It was right around this time that WHAS had a farm and garden director named Barney Arnold and WAVE TV and radio had Jack Crowner serving as their farm and garden director. So I decided to call Barney and Jack and invite them out to our farm. I said, "Let me show you what I've got and run past you the idea that I have." When I explained to them the idea of the U-Pick, they both thought that it was a super idea. Barney made the comment, "Joe, as long as this is a good deal for the consumer I will push it as hard as I can! If it is a matter of putting a dollar in your pocket then I have to back off." These guys were there to help the consumer, and I agreed with that, too. So, they both got on the radio and told the listener "Joe has strawberries to pick. Peas are going to be in next week out at Joe's so you better go pick your peas." They told the people where we were located and how to get here. Both of these guys had TV shows as well, and not only did we get publicity on the radio, but we got on TV! These two gentlemen really helped get us going with this U-Pick idea and they supported it 100 percent.

We had other advertising from two county extension agents named Craig Scifert and Bill Brunmit. Craig and Bill were excited about what was going on here and they came to the farm quite a bit. Then they both started sending out information on flyers to local people all around about getting quality products at a lower price than in the grocery stores. They had information printed in the local newspapers and really pushed the U-Pick business. I have to admit, with all this interest, I knew we had started something that was going to be a big success.

With all the different varieties of fruits and vegetables being grown on the farm, the news media always called me to get information. Numerous articles and pictures were printed in the New Albany *Tribune* and the *Courier-Journal*. They knew I was committed to changing and attempting to grow new types of products and wanted to give the community information so they could grow them as well. I think the commitment that I made to learn more about different vegetables and fruits really helped give credibility to this farm and the products that are grown here today.

Skeptics everywhere

When other farmers in the area started hearing about what was going on here at the farm they thought I had lost my mind. They would say, "Joe, if you let those people come out from the city, they will trample your crops and leave you without any vegetables." They also believed that no one would drive thirty miles just to pick vegetables. They tried to discourage me as much as possible. Even my mother, in the beginning, believed it was a bad idea, but she soon became one of my best salespersons.

Now, Bonnie and I had made the commitment that we were not going to go in and pick the best fruits and vegetables first and let the customer get what was left. We were going to let them pick the absolute best; this was to be a U-Pick operation and nothing else. One neighbor came down and said, "Joe, you're going to blow your entire farm. I can get twenty people to come up here from Arkansas to pick your strawberries; all I've got to do is pick up the phone and they're ready to come." I told him "I'm sorry, but Bonnie and I are going to do it this way." He sat there with tears in his eyes, thinking that I was going to lose my farm. I knew, however, that we weren't going to survive the way things were going and that we had to do something different to make it, and Bonnie backed me up completely. There sure wasn't a whole lot of encouragement from the local farmers when it came to moving to the U-Pick style of farming, but I didn't hesitate to ask people for help in spreading the word, and once the word got out people started coming. I have learned that if you ask someone to help they won't turn you down. That's why this U-Pick thing has done as well as it has. All you have to do is be willing to ask, and people will respond and make life a little bit easier for you.

Growing into success

I can remember those early years being slow, but we were definitely doing much better than we had ever done before. We were raising all kinds of stuff for people to come in and pick. Then in 1971, it hit like a storm, and I couldn't believe how much fruit and vegetables people were picking. People were picking more than we could raise; it was truly amazing. Local people couldn't believe it. They were amazed because, before, we had spent so much time picking and preparing to take the products to the wholesalers, and now people were doing the picking and we were getting paid for it. I think that the people just enjoyed getting out away from the city for the day to have a nice, relaxing time. The community quickly noticed the success that we were having, and that's when my cousin at the Huber Orchard and Winery and the Stumlers asked if I minded if they got involved with the U-Pick business. My response to them was, "There are plenty enough people to go around; all we have to do is have enough sense to work together. Let's cooperate with each other and not be competitors but cooperators."

This type of sharing of success has been going on ever since. We continue to work together, we are all good friends, we support each other, and we support each other's business. If I am out of white sweet corn and at ten o'clock Saturday morning a customer asks me for ten bushels, then I tell them that I'm out and direct them to Huber Orchard or to Stumler's. That way they don't leave Starlight without getting a quality product and they'll want to return again. People don't want to hear you badmouth the other businesses because it just doesn't make you look very professional; that's why cooperation is so important.

During the peak of the U-Pick, Joe III was twenty-one years old and the youngest, Chuck, was eleven years old. The kids really enjoyed the opportunity to get out and show people how to pick the products. When it came to picking strawberries it was important that the customer picked the best products that were available. We didn't want them to pick in an area that someone else had already picked! It was the kids' responsibility to move red surveyor flags to mark the areas that were ready to be picked. As they grew up, they took on more roles with the business. They would help with weighing and collecting the money, answering the telephones and people's questions, and driving the U-Pick trucks out into the fields. We really wanted to supply the customer not only a quality product, but also that personal family touch. My mother would often come out into the fields and offer people lemonade as they picked. She always enjoyed talking with the people; she would even invite them to come into her house to use the restroom if they needed to. With our kids being involved with Bonnie and me, these people really had the opportunity to see a family working together and enjoying what they were doing.

This venture started out as a great financial necessity, but the results were far above what I ever expected would happen. I believe that if we had not changed at that time, we could have ended up not having the farm today. When I was a young man in this community, there were thirty-four fruit and vegetable farmers; today there are four. Back then you had to be a big operation to sell to the places such as Kroger's. We were never big fruit and vegetable growers so we had to find a way to make more with less. We had to find a way that we could sell directly to the consumer, and Pick Your Own was the way it needed to be.

From about 1971 to about 1981, it was tremendous the amount

of people that came here to pick. I remember that in 1974 the national media started saying that there might be a food shortage. People believed that there were not going to be enough canned fruits and vegetables on the shelves to feed their families. The consuming public really panicked and you talk about getting picked out — that's exactly what happened here. We were raising sixty to seventy acres of sweet corn, thirty to thirty-five acres of green beans, thirty-five acres of strawberries, and we had lots of other products as well. I can still see clearly the vision I saw in the fields August 16, 1974. At 10 o'clock in the morning there were seven hundred and thirty two people just in the green bean fields alone, picking as much as they could. That was just the green beans! Man, we had so many people that we just about went crazy. These people were buying deep freezes because they were storing our product in bulk amounts, and we happened to be one of the few U-Pick businesses in the area. During that period of time, you talk about selling. It was something else!

Community help

With all those people here picking, we just couldn't handle it all, so we had to get help from somewhere. That's where Bonnie's sisters Blanche, who worked on the farm for twenty-two years, and Marcella, who worked for about twelve years, came into the picture and really helped out with all the customers. Bonnie and they would spend many nights developing recipes for each item that we grew on the farm so that people didn't leave here without knowing how to prepare and keep the food. Things that they would work on were: how to make apple preserves, how to freeze strawberries, how to can green beans, how to get the corn off the ear, and recipes for everything! It is one thing to read a recipe and cook, but these people had never prepared fresh fruits and vegetables and they had hundreds of questions. Bonnie, along with her sisters, made' sure all those questions didn't go unanswered, and people really appreciated this. One thing that I realized from this was that personal contact with people who had worked much of their lives preparing fresh products for their families was important. You can't have a seventeen-year-old young lady out talking to someone, telling them how to can items, and expect the customer to feel comfortable.

As our farming operation continued to grow, so did our need for land to plant new crops. So, I went to three different neighbors and asked them to lease a portion of their land to me on a five-year lease. You wouldn't believe the cooperation that I got from my neighbors. Now, I paid good money for their land, but the mere fact that they were willing to work with me meant a whole lot. That's what neighbors should be like, willing to help when they're asked. Neighbors helping neighbors has always been important in the Starlight community.

Bonnie's sister Martha is also someone in the community that really helped me out. One Saturday morning I called her up to help me sell over a hundred bushels of potatoes. You see, Martha has a voice that could be heard distinctly over a crowd of people. Well, I told Martha that I was going to put her on the U-Pick truck and as it was going out into the fields she was to say, "Mrs. Huber, you be sure to save me five bushels of potatoes because I'm sure you'll run out!" She planted the seed in every customer that was on the farm, "Hey, Huber's going to run out of potatoes and we need to get them before they do." I'm telling you, talk about selling potatoes, they sold like crazy; the women were coming in from the fields buying bushels at a time. Before noon we sold a hundred and sixty bushels of potatoes.

One of our first U-Pick customers, Helen Silverman, became a great friend and help to our family when we were just starting. Helen was sixty-seven her first trip to the farm and returned each year till 1993. She has always called me "Poppy" and took interest in Bonnie and the family from the beginning. She would come and pick twice a week and often would bring us lunch so that Bonnie didn't have to cook and could relax. Helen taught for many years at Spalding, and she often offered good advice. The relationship we shared has always been special and her caring cherished. Thanks, Helen!

Bonnie and customers

When these big crowds came over here to pick all those vegetables and fruits, Bonnie was the person that would talk to them and make sure they were happy. She was the person that helped weigh the product, collect the money, answer the phone, and she was always going a hundred miles an hour, cooking, cleaning, plus raising five kids. Bonnie has a super personality! If you put Bonnie with another lady on a one-on-one basis they will have a conversation that is really something. That lady could come up and tell Bonnie her name and Bonnie would never forget it. Bonnie might have a conversation in which a lady would tell her that her granddaughter has been sick, and that lady would come back a year later to pick and Bonnie would ask her by her first name how her granddaughter was doing. Do you know what that means to people, to be called by their name after a year's time and to have someone remember personal things that were going on in their lives? Boy, that really impresses people because they know that you are genuinely interested in them. Bonnie has always been dedicated like that about other people. She wants to know everybody! Bonnie is the person that made the U-Pick a success with her dedication to the people.

Opportunity of a lifetime

The U-Pick gave us the opportunity to keep our family together working here on the farm. When it grew like it did, my kids had the opportunity to stay here on the farm and not have to work anywhere else. On most farms the children have to go into town and find a job, but that wasn't the way we wanted it and it wasn't the way it worked out. Also, U-Pick helped put the community of Starlight on the map and it helped a lot of other families start up businesses as well. Most of the businesses here in Starlight are family owned and operated, such as Stumler's and Huber Orchard and Winery. These operations, as well as ours, are into the third generation of family as the owners. That family ownership means a lot to a man and his wife who have worked a farm all of their lives, to see their children take it over. Farming takes great commitment and a great amount of work, but it's all worth it when family can stay together and continue traditions.

In 1981, with the great decline of the economy, we saw a significant change here in Starlight as well. Households came into hard times, and this is when the housewives, looking for additional family income, went to work. This really took away from our customer base and we decided it was time to start picking and selling directly from our farm in our Country Store. People still wanted a fresh product and enjoyed the drive out to the farm, but they had no time to pick. So, we started picking it for them and sold it at the farm market. With all this picking, we had to work sixty to seventy kids during the summer to help pick the products so we would have enough to sell. I even bought a pea sheller so that the customers didn't have to spend time shelling the peas themselves.

Bonnie was busy running the Country Store and keeping things together for the family. She made small recipe books to go along with items that were being sold. These books cost about sixteen cents each to make, and that first year we must have given over 60,000 away. The next year we decided to charge a quarter and we still sold over 60,000. The family was busy helping out on the farm by raising fifty-one varieties of fruits and vegetables and helping run the store. Lots of change was going on, but we worked hard to keep the family generating enough money to keep everyone here on the farm.

I was busy out in the fields farming and deciding what needed to be picked and how much. I became the public-relations man, making commercials, telling people about what was going on here at the farm. This is about the time that I started a good friendship with Fred Wiche, who had become WHAS's farm and garden director, and starting doing commercials with him on the radio. It didn't take us long to develop a close tie and Fred and his wife Jenny really became close friends of ours. Fred helped us out a lot in talking up the fruits and vegetables that we were picking at this time. It was a challenge because we weren't used to having to prepackage items to keep them fresh. I tell you what helped us continue our success; it was that personal touch we put into everything that we were doing. I believe that if we had lost that touch with the changes, we wouldn't have made it farming those next few years.

Bonnie, listening to the customers, found people came to the farm and spent so much time enjoying the day that they were constantly asking if she had any food to eat. This is when Bonnie started serving food, and people really enjoyed being able to eat while at the farm. So, Bonnie started serving people on a regular basis in the Country Store with things such as soup, sandwiches, and homemade pies. Right around that same time, my sons started providing hayrides on the weekends to customers for their enjoyment. So, I decided that we were becoming much more than a farm. We were becoming family entertainment!

Recipe:

Short Cake

2 cups flour   4 tbsp. butter
1/4 cup sugar   1 egg
1 tsp. baking powder   1/2 cup milk
pinch of salt

Combine dry ingredients and cut in butter. Mix egg and milk, add to other ingredients and mix with hands to form dough. Press into a pie plate. Bake at 375° until lightly browned.

Slice and sugar strawberries to your taste. Spoon over shortcake. Top with whipped cream.

Whipped cream
1 pint whipping cream   1 tsp. vanilla
1 tbsp. sugar

Whip cream, adding other ingredients.

Makes a beautiful and delicious short cake.

Joe Huber Family Restaurant.

8

Putting It on the Line

As I mentioned, the early '80s saw a tremendous change in our customers' lifestyles. The average housewife left the home to go to work, and people began looking for quicker ways for the family to enjoy dinner together. They started eating out more and not cooking at home as much. We found that Bonnie had a tremendous thing going in the Country Store with all the customers asking her to feed them, and she really enjoyed cooking for them. Not only did she enjoy it, they did as well; and they waited in line patiently for Bonnie's homemade soups, pies, cobblers, sandwiches, and other items. There became a greater demand for her cooking than that lunchroom could handle, and we really weren't set up right to serve food. Bonnie was working so hard to feed people it was becoming a big challenge, so I started looking around this farm trying to think of a way that we might change to meet the needs of our customers. Then in 1982 I said to myself, "Maybe we should build a restaurant right here on the farm!"

That same year at Christmas break, Chuck, our youngest child, came home from Purdue and said, "I want to become involved with what is going on here on the farm." Chuck's involvment would mean that all five of our children wanted to be working on the farm. Joe III and Louie were doing a super job with U-Pick, and Bonnie with Beverly and Kimmy had things working well in the Country Store. I believe that we were all searching for a new challenge and a way to keep everyone in the family here on the farm. All we needed was a bigger piece of pie to meet the financial needs for our family. Our children were young and they needed something that could motivate them, something that they could get their teeth into. They had to believe that they had some ownership and responsibility to make it happen, no matter what it was. I believe that what we do in our lives has to be something we enjoy doing; plus, there has to be some challenge for it to seem exciting. I freed myself up and began brainstorming about the idea of a family farm restaurant. I quickly realized that we needed it for a service to our customers and as a financial necessity. We knew the customers needed and wanted it, but we had to want it ourselves.

Moving to bigger things

I don't know if people realized that I was serious when I kept saying that we were going to build a restaurant, but I kept telling myself that we could do it! Before anything was to get started, I had to find out if we could get the proper zoning for a restaurant out in the country. This was a new idea, and we were definitely breaking new ground with it. It took several meetings with the county commissioners and the planning and zoning board explaining to them what our idea was and the concepts behind it. I emphasized how we would be an asset to the community because of the employment that we would be able to provide to those who lived nearby. I didn't care what their talents were or how old they were, we had a job for them. During lots of family meetings, we discussed the importance of being an asset to the community. We have always taken into consideration the importance of neighbors, family, and friends. This same philosophy was taken to the county commissioners and planning and zoning boards to help us get the permits that we needed to build.

Once we got the permits, we were ready to start the serious planning. The family met often to get everybody's comments and suggestions regarding this new venture. The main thing that Bonnie and I were looking for was the commitment, "Hey, we want to do this, we will stay here with it, and we will make this thing happen!" We had to have total commitment from our family to make this thing work. In these meetings we would talk about who was going to run the kitchen, who was going to be the person who managed the dining room. I believed that if one person could manage the kitchen and one person could manage the dining room then things would run a lot smoother. We continued to meet and things really started to jell. Right around that time, Louie declared, "I'll go for it and run that kitchen!" and Katie, Louie's wife, said, "And I'll manage the dining room." The restaurant had begun to take shape.

Planning it out

Now, we had a lot of advice from local people, family, and others, but someone that really helped plan out this restaurant was a man named Jim Smith who owned and operated The Wheel Restaurant in Sellersburg. Bonnie and I were good customers at this place; we went there three or four times a month. Jim had this restaurant set up sit-down style, where the waitresses would come and take care of you. I really wanted to have a place where you could come in, sit down, relax, and let some one else take care of you. So I asked Jim all kinds of questions about how we should start out and what we needed to do. I made up my mind that our restaurant was going to be a place that took extremely good care of people and listened to their concerns. It was going to be a place that the whole family could enjoy without worrying about fixing any food, or if it was going to be good or not. Most people work hard for somebody else all week long, and they need to feel like they are the boss once in a while. There is no better place than a restaurant like the one I was planning for someone to come in, be the boss, and make all the decisions. I wanted a place where someone could get away and not worry about the city life and all its hustling around. I wanted a place that was going to offer them great food and good scenery (no looking out the window and seeing a parking lot), that was a place for the whole family.

With all these thoughts put together, we finally broke ground, and I will never, ever forget that day as long as I live. First of all, the day was April 1st —April Fool's day — 1983; what fools we were to be breaking ground on that day! Then there was the part that really made things worse! The previous night we had a pretty hard freeze. We'd had an early spring, and at that time we had over 2,700 peach trees on the farm, not to mention all the other fruit trees. The irrigation system we had running on the strawberries froze solid that night. The day that we broke ground we lost most of our peaches and a lot of other products, and that cost us a whole lot of money. So, here we were getting ready to make a heck of a financial investment and we had just lost a whole bunch. You talk about tough! That was tough! I had knots in my stomach all morning long just thinking about all that had happened. We went right on with our ceremony, which included the entire family, my mother, my brother Norbert, and the local parish priest, who gave the blessing on that ground. As soon as that was over, the contractor was right there ready to start backhoeing the ground to move right along.

We hired a local contractor, Starlight Construction (two brothers, whom our family knew very well) to build the restaurant. Now, the deal we had was that my three boys, Jo Jo, Louie, and Chuck, would help with as much of the work as possible to keep the cost down. These boys drove a lot of nails during that time and it was something else watching all the work that went into the preparation of the restaurant. The role I played in all this construction was making sure that all the details went just right. As it went up, I would sit there visualizing how things would look, how the traffic flow of people going in and out would be, moving the location of doorways, and thinking of the ways that we could expand if we needed to. Throughout the building process, there was never any doubt that we would succeed. I never doubted that Bonnie and our family would make this work, because our family made a commitment and we were sincere. I can remember my parents always preaching, "You can do anything," to us when we were children, and my experience in life has proven that they were right. One of my mother's favorite sayings was, "To do something, you have to want to do it. Then you can do it." I wanted to build that restaurant! We all wanted to make it happen!

There were plenty of other things that we had to think about before we opened our doors to the public. The first thing that I learned was that you had better come up with a good menu, and then you can feed people. After we had the menu, then we could worry about other things. It didn't take very long for us to come up with a menu because Bonnie had become a great cook and she had plenty of recipes for meats, vegetables, and especially desserts. Once we got the menu taken care of, we talked with consultants about what we needed to do with our kitchen. This was quite an ordeal because we ordered our kitchen items from a local distributor in the city and it took them quite a long time to get us our supplies. The items all required a deposit that I had put down to ensure delivery. I became very frustrated when they took twice as long to deliver as they had told us they would. I learned that city folk often talk a good sell but can't deliver the items when they are supposed to, and from that time on I have never purchased a product if I had to put down a deposit. If I order something, I'm going to pay for it when it comes. All of the suppliers that I have used made a commitment to our family to give us good service and the best products on time, and they are paid upon delivery. We have never shopped on the basis of price, but on the basis of quality and service, and we have remained committed to purchasing from those who have made those same commitments to us.

Bonnie had two sisters, Irma and Marcella, who really knew how to cook, and they came up to help us plan for the opening. Marcella, whom they called Sis, had eleven children, and Irma had ten children. Having that many children, they knew how to prepare in large amounts and they showed us what we needed to do. They said that they would be happy to help us get things going and we were very fortunate to have that kind of expertise. You don't know how much it meant to us to have that type of support from family. Even today, if you come to our restaurant, don't be surprised if you find that the people who are working there are part of our family.

Stepping on new ground

I guess you can say there were many other things that went into planning this restaurant, but one thing that I really wanted was to be able to have a liquor license so that we could serve beer, wine, and other drinks. Now, we knew up front that we weren't going to serve a whole lot of liquor because we were going to have a family restaurant, but this was something that I wanted to offer to our customers. We wanted to be careful to make sure that we didn't become a local hangout for rednecks, and so we priced our liquor high to keep them from coming in. Here again, we found that we were breaking new ground because we wanted to sell liquor out in the country. There are a lot of laws and regulations that control the locations of liquor sales in the county, and I found out that there are only a set number of liquor licenses given out every year. I never dreamed that I would get the license, but I get lucky every once in a while. The day I went in to turn in my application, they had just stripped someone else of their license because they had been serving to minors. It was a first come basis, and it was pure luck that I was that next person to walk through those doors.

Before I even considered applying for the liquor license, I wanted to find out if my neighbors in the community had any objections. We were going to be very conscious of our neighbors' feelings about what we did. I decided that I would ask them to sign a petition in order to get their true feelings about our having a liquor license. I sent out this petition in a one mile radius of our farm and I visited each and every household to find out how they felt about us having a liquor license. I talked to one hundred and sixty two people and everybody signed it except one person, who exclaimed that it didn't make any difference if we had it or not. I believe that the people around here knew that I was someone who had credibility and could be counted on to make sure that it would remain controlled.

Knowing that we were risking it all financially, I planned things very carefully here on the farm. Jo Jo was busy running the farm, Bonnie and the girls were busy with the farm market, and Louie and Chuck were keeping things together with the U-Pick business. Things continued to run smoothly; that was the way it had to be with everybody in the family working. We weren't working 8:00 a.m. to 5:00 p.m.; we worked from the morning till it got dark, doing our regular business and then driving nails in the evening.

There were an awful lot of risks building a restaurant without having any experience. All of our family, at all of those meetings, gathered all the facts that we could so that we could make an intelligent decision. Bonnie and I put everything that we owned on the line to build this restaurant. Another risk was that we were building a restaurant seven miles off a state highway in the middle of the country. I know that I had never seen anyone build a restaurant that far away from a big community, and for that reason nobody knew if it would be successful or not. Sure, we heard all the statistics that indicated that 90 percent of all restaurants go broke in the first year, but we just were listening to what our customers wanted. If you go out to the Hurstborne Lane area all you see is restaurants changing names and reopening under new management. Something that alleviated our risk is that we were well known through the U-Pick operation; people knew who the Joe Huber family was. We weren't starting from scratch because we had that name recognition and people already knew how to get to our farm.

Opening the doors

The first experience we had opening the restaurant was on July 14, 1983, when we invited the members of Bonnie's family and my family to eat at the restaurant. We had forty-two people come to eat, and at the end of the night we gave each of them a comment card to fill out. I begged them not to say we did fine, but to pick us apart so that we would know what we were doing wrong and what we needed to do to make it better. I told them that we would give them a dinner, but that in turn they had to be truthful to me in these comments. Well, we made several mistakes, and there were things we did that we shouldn't have done, but our plan was to open our doors again the second night to the local neighbors to give it a second try. We had about a hundred and seventy neighbors that night, and again we asked them to give us their comments. We found that it went a whole lot smoother the second night, and that really helped.

So we actually opened the restaurant on a Wednesday, July 16, 1983, and we did this without any advertising except a sign while the restaurant was being built that stated, "Opening July 16." We thought that we might get a hundred and forty to a hundred and sixty people to come and eat dinner, but it turned out that we had three hundred and sixty seven people come to eat. We served about all the food that we had at lunch alone, and we still had to get ready for dinner! We couldn't seat everybody because we were completely full, and people were out front waiting. Fortunately, we had called a lot of family to help us out that first night and people left happy. We made it happen. Needless to say, though, this was a lot more than we expected to happen, and changes had to be made quickly because we stayed busy and didn't have much of a slowdown.

We quickly realized that we didn't really know what we had gotten ourselves into and needed some help. To make matters better, but worse, the *Courier-Journal* sent a critic up here, and I never will forget the headlines: "Our Critic's Dream Come True." We received a three-and-a-half star rating out of a possible four, and after that, you talk about getting bombed with people! It was unreal the numbers of people who came here. So I called Shirley Nolot, a good friend and neighbor who was the Cafeteria Manager at Borden High School, to come up here to help us to cook in greater volumes. She and her assistant had experience working with big groups, and they taught us the best ways to serve people in large volumes. Next, Louie found out that the kitchen needed to be changed drastically from the stuff that the supplier had given us to something he could be more comfortable with. Finally, we learned that we were going to have to have someone help us train our waitresses, and that is where Alice Green, a close friend of ours, helped out. She had a lot of experience and knew how things should be done, and she demanded perfection from those waitresses, many of whom were part of our family. She was one of the greatest things that ever happened to us!

Other things we had to be aware of were: the cost of running a restaurant and really being efficient, using time right, not being wasteful, and understanding our customers. I quickly found out that I was going to have to build on to the restaurant and put in a better parking area, because people wanted a paved parking lot instead of a white rock gravel parking lot, and we needed more space. Following the *Courier-Journal's* article, we had a different clientele than expected and we definitely needed to do a lot of work to meet their needs. Bonnie really came to the forefront because she could relate to these people much better than I could, and she spent hours and hours talking with people. She also got together with our daughters, and they spent hours picking out flowers and other items, decorating to make the place perfect.

A bigger step

Things went really well for us with the restaurant, and people continued to come back as an annual tradition for Easter, Mother's Day, Father's Day, and many other events. People were always calling asking if we would be able to accommodate really large groups, and we started having companies calling trying to reserve for outings. We started thinking about doing company picnics; but I think it really started when Toro Lawn Company had a convention in Louisville and a lady called and said she had heard about our restaurant, and that they would like to come out to eat. I naturally said, "Wonderful, we would be glad to have you. How many do you have in your group?" She responded that they had six hundred people. I knew that there was no way we could handle that large a group in the restaurant, so I told her that it wasn't possible. Sure enough, that same lady called the next day asking if there was any way we could have them over. They wanted to come the next day, so I called the family together and said that we would rent a tent and serve them buffet style. We had to figure in the cost of renting the tent, getting the chairs, and all sorts of other things to get it ready overnight. We made it happen, and they came out on some buses they had rented. We expected them to be casually dressed. When they stepped off those buses they were in suits, white shirts, and ties. My three boys and I sat there and said, "This is going to be a disaster," because all we had was a tent, a grassy area, and a place where they could sit down and eat. Those buses kept coming and the crowd kept getting bigger and bigger, so big that I told my oldest son Joe to hook up a bunch of tractors and trailers and haul them away.

Once we got people going on those hayrides, they started spreading out, and the next thing we noticed the ties were coming off and people started loosening up and having a ball. They played volleyball, drank a little beer and wine, and ate plenty of food, and finally things started winding down. My son Joe figured up the bill and it came to something over $10,000, which absolutely blew our minds. Joe came to me and said, "I can't take them this bill. These people are going to have a fit! What am I going to do?" I said, "Now, I told them how much everything was going to be, but we didn't figure how much they were going to use, so give them the bill." Joe folded the bill and put it in an envelope so he could give it to the lady and hopefully get away before she opened it. She opened it, though, folded it up, and asked, "Would it be all right if we mailed you a check?" Joe said, "That'll be fine." She never made any comment and two weeks later we received their check. They even added a $1,000 tip and a letter stating how much they enjoyed the time they had on the farm, and our family. It was time to start doing company picnics!

We realized that not only were we a place that served great food and sold quality fruits and vegetables, but we were also a place of entertainment. We built two company picnic facilities for people to use, and they have started using our barnyard bash areas so much that we can book them almost a year in advance. This has given my son Chuck and his wife Tracye an opportunity to manage the company picnics through the farm. We put in horseshoe pits, volleyball courts, basketball courts, a playground, softball fields, lakes with ducks and fish, and hayrides around the farm. My nephew Dan Schmidt is the person that takes groups for a ride around the farm, and he really captivates them with his stories and jokes. People enjoy the stories so much that they often ride around twice.

One thing we have found about our farm: people enjoy getting out into the country and being able to see the trees, flowers, and plants. We have over 1,700 varieties of day lilies, and when the more than 200,000 day lily plants on the farm are in bloom from June through September they are really something to see. Garden clubs, church groups, and all kinds of people come out here to see our flowers and plants. I have found myself getting really involved with wildflowers; that is kind of my new thing that I really enjoy. Families can come out and see how fruits and vegetables are planted and raised and can learn more about how to grow them on one of our tours around the farm.

In the fall of the year we don't have a special fall festival; every day is a fall festival! We have German bands playing, a chuck wagon style buffet, pumpkin picking, hayrides, storytelling, and much more. For families to drive sixty miles to come and eat means that we are doing things right. People can enjoy themselves no matter what age they are here at the farm because they can take part in watching their children and grandchildren having a good time.

One thing I learned is that when our children have a good day, then we are in a good mood, and that is what is most important in our lives: watching our children grow up and have a good time. I spend a lot of time watching families to see what makes them happy, because what we want to do is make this farm a place that is fun for people's families. You see, what we have realized is that this farm is not just our farm, it is a family farm, and I don't mean my immediate family, but a family of friends. Everybody that has continued to come out here over the years has become part of our family, and that has meant more to me than you can imagine.

What it has meant

The farm, restaurant, and company picnics have meant a lot of things. The biggest thing is that they have allowed us to be on the farm working together as a family. We have watched our children build their homes here, and our endeavors have given them the one thing that Bonnie and I wanted for ourselves — for them to be able to work with their own brothers, sisters, and children, and to have the chance to stay close to family. Our children have the opportunity to go home during the day and be with their kids. It was a dream come true for Bonnie and me that we had started a family business and the pie was big enough that it could support all the members. It gave the members of our family the chance to use all of their different talents and it has been rewarding to watch our children, sons-in-law, daughters-in-law, and grandchildren putting these talents to use. It was a challenge to make this farm work and it really pulled us together and helped us to understand the importance of communicating and expressing our feelings to each other. We learned more about each other and our personalities so that we could appreciate everybody in this entire family. We met a challenge and won with family. They didn't make it succeed, and Bonnie and I didn't make it succeed, but it was together that our family made it succeed, and it couldn't have worked any other way.

Recipe:

Oven Fried Chicken

1 cup flour	2 tsp. paprika
2 tsp. salt	1 cut up fryer
1/4 tsp. pepper	1/2 cup shortening and butter

Heat oven to 425°. Mix flour, salt, pepper, and paprika in paper bag. Put shortening and butter in a 13 x 9-1/2 x 2-inch pan and set in oven to melt. Shake three or four pieces of chicken at a time in bag to coat thoroughly. Place chicken skin side down in a single layer in hot shortening. Bake 30 minutes, turn skin side up and bake 30 minutes more or until chicken is done.

The children today — from left, Joe III, Beverly, Joe, Bonnie, Louie, Kimmy, and Chuck.

9
Our Children

O ur oldest son is Joe III, and he was in the last graduating class at Flaget High School in Louisville. It was quite a challenge for us to send him over there, because we didn't have the time to take him and pick him up and he didn't have a driver's license. So, he had to catch a ride every day to and from school. It all worked out, though, and he graduated and then went on to Purdue University, where he majored in economics and agronomy.

I never will forget the day that we took him to the university. We took him up to the dormitory where he was going to be staying and unloaded him and all his clothes. We left him a bicycle, because he wasn't allowed to have a car up there, and as we were leaving, Bonnie and I looked out the back window at our little boy. He had a long, sad face as he was waving good-bye, and that was just about too much for us to handle. Here was our own flesh and blood, and we just "dropped him off." I guess we were both crying, but Bonnie was really crying, and she thought it was just terrible that I would do such a thing to him. She was really after me: "Turn around, let's take him home!" But I said we couldn't do that and we came on home.

He did well in school, though, and when he graduated, Bonnie and I encouraged him to go someplace else to get a job so that he could make sure that this farm was where he wanted to be. So, he went to work as a farm manager for a packing company in Franklin, Indiana (about a hundred miles north of here), where he raised and processed three hundred and fifty acres of tomatoes. He stayed there for one year, and he really enjoyed it. He didn't come home too often because he was so busy, but in the fall of the year, when things slowed down, he was coming home every weekend, and I told Bonnie, "It's not going to be too long until we hear Joe ask about coming back here with us." In November of that year, he said, "I'll tell you what, I want to come back. I want to be here on this farm with you." Of course, that just tickled us to death, and when he came back, he bought himself a fifteen-acre farm right up the road, and he and his wife Kathy put a new mobile home on it. They lived there about two years, and then he built his new home on our farm, where he's living now.

When Joe and Kathy got married, my son Louie was going to be his best man. The night before their wedding we had a rehearsal dinner, and after it, Louie and my future son-in-law, Kenny, had an automobile accident on the way home in which Louie got his right ankle broken. Well, he couldn't be in the wedding the next day, so I stood in as the best man. Of course, Louie was in the hospital with a big cast on his leg, so the whole wedding party went there to see him. He was laying in bed with his tuxedo on and we all signed his cast, but the thing we found most amusing was that every room in the hospital that we went by had somebody in it call out, "Hey, we want to see the bride!" So, that got to be a pretty long stay, with Kathy going in and showing off her dress to everybody. In a way, it was rough, but overall I think it was a good experience, although Louie might disagree!

Joe and Kathy now have three children. Their oldest, Joe IV, is twenty years old, and he manages what we call the packing shed of our farm market. He washes and pre-packages all the fruits and vegetables before they go out for sale in our store. Their next, Terra, is fourteen years old. She's involved in doing a lot of the computer work for Joe and Kathy in their business of the Starlight Day Lily Gardens. Their younger daughter is Jenna, and she's eight years old.

Kimmy

Next in line is Kim. She started high school at Loretta High school in Louisville, but that closed down after her freshman year, so she transferred to Providence High School in Clarksville. When she graduated from Providence she went on to Indiana University Southeast, and when she finished there she traveled back to Louisville to get her master's degree in speech and hearing therapy. Today, Kim is the Director of the

Speech and Hearing Department at Bridgepoint, which is a facility in Clarksville that works with children who have hearing and speech impediments. Kim and I often talk about how my mother would tell us kids, "You've got to stand up straight, put your head back, and learn to E-NUN-CI-ATE," so we think that it's kind of a natural rub-off for Kim to be helping other children to speak more clearly and plainly.

When we were all on the farm here, Kim spent most of her time in the house, because Bonnie was usually in the fields with us. So, Kimmy was the one who was doing most of the cooking, keeping the house clean, and all of that kind of stuff. Back then, Kim would fix lunch for us every day. She was around thirteen years old at this time, and her idea of lunch was taking a bunch of sliced bologna, throwing it in a pan under the broiler, putting a little barbecue sauce on it, and slicing and frying a little squash to go with it on the side. Every day it was the same thing, barbecued bologna and fried squash. We got so tired of that stuff, we thought we were going to die. Well, today we have the restaurant, and we get so tired of fried chicken that we look forward to a little barbecued bologna every now and then. We have it every once in a while, too, and it brings back a lot of good memories.

When Kim got married, she wanted to have her wedding reception in the Barnyard Bash Company Picnic building, so we had a florist come in to decorate that particular building, which is seventy feet by one hundred feet on the inside. On each end of the building, he constructed a twelve-foot waterfall, and the flowers you wouldn't believe! What he did inside that building was almost miraculous! We had never seen anything as elegant as the inside of that building was for Kimberly's wedding.

Kim is expecting her first child in August 1995. It'll be Bonnie's and my twelfth grandchild, and we're very excited about that. Kim's husband, Mike, is also involved in a business with his dad and their family, so he really understands what family means to us. Neither Kimmy nor her husband works here on the farm full-time, but during strawberry season in the spring and pumpkin season in the fall those two are here every Saturday and Sunday helping our family through the busy weekends, and we really appreciate that.

Beverly

Next in the line of our children is Beverly, and she always was the most competitive of all our children. She grew up playing basketball in our packing shed against Joe, Louie and Chuck, and it got to be kind of a rough and tumble thing with her. When she started high school at Providence, she went out for their basketball team and made the girl's varsity squad in her freshman year. The first game that she played, she scored thirty-two points, and she fouled out in the fourth quarter with about five minutes to go!

She had girls laying all over that floor. When she went up for a rebound, if a girl came down on her, that girl's butt hit the floor! The referees would call time out and they'd caution Beverly about how rough she was playing. The opposing coach was raising the devil, so the refs also were talking to him, and talking to Beverly's coach, who in turn was talking to Beverly again. "Slow down! You've got to slow down," they would say. It was a mess. So, when the game was all over with, Beverly's coach came to over to talk to me, and she told me, "Mr. Huber, you've got to talk to that girl! She can't play ball like that. She's too rough!" I said, "That's the way she was raised; that's her competitive spirit. I'll tell you something, I will talk to her because you've asked me too, but you'll ruin her as a basketball player," and they did. She started playing like the rest of the girls and she never again scored anywhere near the number of points that she did her first night. I asked her coach, "What do you care if she fouls out of the game? If she gets you thirty-two points, that ought to satisfy you!" That was just her competitive spirit shining through.

Another thing that happened when the kids were little, I don't know how it got started, but Joe and Louie got to teasing Beverly one day, calling her "groundhog." That nickname stuck with her, and Joe even wrote a song about her:

"Beverly was a groundhog, loved to have her fun.
She's a deep hole digger (scared of dogs)
and a root-eating son of a gun!"

He'd sing that song to her, and it's got to where it's going on even today. On Groundhog Day, Beverly gets birthday cards from all of her brothers and sisters. Of course, they don't sign them, it's all "incognito," but she knows who's sending them, and that'll probably stick with her the rest of her life.

100

When Beverly got married — of course, women decide all these things — but when she got married she had us men wear bright yellow tuxedos. Beverly's father-in-law is a pretty good sized man, like myself, and everybody was kidding us, calling us the "Canary Twins." I guess we did look like two canaries running around there.

At one time, Beverly worked at a bank, but that only lasted for about eight months until she decided that she couldn't stay cooped up inside all day long. Then she came on back to the farm. Now, she and her husband, Kenny, manage our farm market and our gift shop, and we're glad they're here! Beverly now has two children, Jason, who is seventeen, and Brittany, who's thirteen, both of whom are now enrolled at Providence High School.

Louie

Next is Louie. His name's Lewis, but he's always been Louie to us. It sounds kind of tough to do this, but we had a dog around here at one point in time and we name him Louie, and when Lewis was born, we named him after the dog! People don't believe it, but that's really the way it happened!

Anyhow, he went to Providence High School, and when he graduated, his mother and I really encouraged him to go onto college, but school was not his thing. He didn't enjoy school, and he said, "Everything that I need to know in life, you can teach me, because I have every intention of staying here on this farm." He's the most impatient of all our children. He doesn't have time to talk about what we're going to do. When you mention it, Louie's ready to go do it! "Let's go for it," that's always been his saying. He would ask, "Why should I waste four years of my life and your money going to school, when all I really want to do is work here?" So, Louie's been working here ever since.

When Louie and Katie were married, it was quite a day. Again, the women all decided that the men should wear white tuxedos. Now, Katie's father is a pretty heavyset man, like myself, but he's fun-loving and he felt it would be appropriate if he and I were both to wear white top hats and carry white canes. So, we did, and it didn't take long for people to start kidding us about how much we looked like Boss Hogg, who was quite a character on the TV show "The Dukes of Hazzard!"

Louie and Katie have four children. Their oldest one is Abby, and she is twelve years old. Their next is Amy, who is nine. Lewis, Jr., is four years old and their baby is Lucas, who is now two years old. They certainly have their hands full, because Louie is in charge of the kitchen in the restaurant, and Katie oversees the dining room. Fortunately, they both live close by so that they can be with their children whenever they need to be, either at home, or at work.

Chuck

Our youngest child is Charles, but everybody around here calls him Chuck. When we moved from the new house down to the farm back in 1967, Chuck was only two years old. Being that young, home to him was still up on the corner in the new house where Mother and Dad were now living. He'd get Kimmy by the hand and try to drag her up the road because he wanted to go home, and that was a tough thing for Bonnie to go through back then when we traded houses. He eventually came through it OK, though.

One year at our Starlight Strawberry Festival, he met his wife, Tracye. You see, we always have a queen contest, and this particular year she was a contestant. The night before the actual contest, we had a dance where you could buy tickets to dance with the queen contestants to raise a little money for the church, and I bought a bunch of tickets just to help contribute. Well, I was out on the floor dancing with all these contestants, and when I finally got around to dancing with Tracye, we'd probably danced less than ten seconds before Chuck came and tapped me on the shoulder, saying, "I believe this is one, Dad, that I ought to take care of." That's how they met, and of course they went on to get married.

When he and Trayce were married, it was a fun wedding. Tracye's grandfather is a Baptist minister, and he officiated at the ceremony, which added a lot to it. After the wedding ceremony, I had arranged for a horse and buggy to take them from the church to the reception, and Tracye really got a kick out of that. Even though she was born and raised in Louisville, everything about the country intrigued her. It was a short ride, only about three city blocks or so, but that helped make their wedding a neat experience for everybody who was involved with it. Now they have two children: Samantha, who we've nicknamed Sam, is eight years old, and Clinton is four.

Chuck attended Purdue University for a while, but then he really fell in love with flying. He's worked hard at that. He's done it all on his own time and now he has his commercial flying license. He does a lot of charter work, and he also donates quite a bit of time to the Kentucky Organ Doner Association. He'll fly doctors around to different cities to pick up transplant organs, and I believe that's kind of his way of giving back a little bit.

1967-1981

At this time, we were still raising a lot of fruits and vegetables commercially for the market, along with operating the Pick Your Own farm, and it wasn't unusual for us to raise thirty acres of cucumbers and about fifteen acres of peppers. We would pick and run through our packing shed semi loads of cucumbers every day. Bonnie and our four children (Kimmy was working in the house), along with some of the neighborhood kids that we would hire to help, would pack twelve to fifteen hundred cartons of cucumbers (twenty four cucumbers in a carton) every day. They also had to pack five to six hundred bushels of peppers. They did a lot of work, but we were all working together, so it was still a lot of fun.

I never will forget one evening; we had a great big order for cucumbers and peppers, and even though it was about seven o'clock, we hadn't stopped for supper. We were all getting hungry, and Louie came up with the idea that we really ought to have us some White Castles. I said that'd be fine and I reached in my pocket, pulled out a wad of money, I have no idea how much it was, but I handed it to Louie and said, "Here. You go get 'em." He took off to the New Albany White Castle. Counting the neighborhood kids, there were only about fourteen of us working. Well, Louie came home with three hundred White Castles along with all the french fries and Cokes to go with it, and we ate every bit of that stuff, cleaned it out! We often reminisce about the night we ate three hundred White Castles.

Anyway, a lot of these cucumbers and peppers that we were picking ourselves we ended up hauling, and I was primarily driving the truck at that time because my boys weren't old enough to be out on the road doing that. I was working all day and driving the truck all night. Whenever I went to Fort

Wayne, I would leave home at midnight, get up there around four o'clock in the morning, and it would be eight o'clock before I could get unloaded. So, I could catch two or three hours of sleep in the truck after I got up there, and that's all the sleep I would get. I'd get back home around noon, and by the time I got home, Bonnie and the kids would have already been in the fields around five hours. They'd have so much already picked that we'd have to go into the packing shed and start packing them!

Bonnie has really done some work on this farm. One day when I was gone, it had rained hard and, I mean to tell you, it was muddy. We had farm trailers at this time that were twenty-five feet long, and we would pour all our cucumbers out loose on the trailers right in the fields. We could get about four hundred bushels on a trailer, and that many weighed about ten tons. Well, this particular day, it was so muddy that they literally buried the trailer in the middle of the field, and Bonnie really had to lead those children. "Come on, we've got to get this thing out of here before Daddy gets home! We've got to be ready to start packing when he gets back!" Bonnie and those kids carried four hundred bushels of cucumbers from the middle of that field out to the road just so they could get them to the packing shed by the time I got back. She is literally a super-woman. It's just unreal the work she has done, but she's never once complained about it.

Getting away

Every year, during this time, Bonnie and I took our children to Florida during their Christmas break from school. During the summer months, our kids were working and they didn't get the chance to go camping and fishing, or swimming. So, we made the commitment to take them on vacation every year so that they could have the time they needed to have a little fun. We didn't have a whole lot of money to work with back then, but Bonnie had a sister, Norma, who lived down in Cocoa, Florida, and we'd stay with her and her husband Carl and their seven boys, and go to Cocoa Beach. Their sons were the same age as our children, and we'd all run around together. Every day, all day long, we'd spend time with our kids on the beach, or fishing, and we really had a lot of fun on those vacations.

One year, I was surf fishing, and I caught a little shark that was about three-and-a-half feet long. Its dorsal fin stood up about seven or eight inches tall, and when I caught it, I tied a string on the end of its tail. Well, I gave it to my kids. They'd run around in the water with that little thing and lead it into a group of people or other families out there playing, then they'd all point and scream,"SHARK! SHARK!" Boy, people would almost walk on the water trying to get of there! They dragged that poor shark around all day, but we had a lot of laughs with it.

We went and stayed with Carl and Norma probably twelve years straight, but in 1984, we started going to Fort Meyers Beach. All our kids were married by then, they were starting to have their own children, and I could afford to rent five condominiums all in the same complex. We'd go down there for two weeks, and you talk about a family having some fun together! We had an absolute ball! We'd rent these great big party boats, and since we had some cousins down in Fort Meyers, there would be as many as fifty or sixty Hubers on a boat at a time, and we'd all grill steaks and do some fishing. Our kids worked hard for us during the rest of the year, and we made a commitment to take them to Florida so that they could play hard, too. Those two week vacations were "anything goes," and it was a great time. We haven't been able to go for the last two years or so because of other commitments, but I believe that this coming year or the next, we're all going to be able to be back together again. We know we can't do it every year anymore, but I think we're going to try to do it every three years, and I think that it'll be absolutely wonderful.

Daredevils

You also wouldn't believe the number of Honda motorcycles and four-wheelers we went through during this time on the farm. One year, I bought the kids a Honda dune buggy, and that was a neat little thing. It would run about thirty-five or forty miles an hour, and it looked like a miniature racer. In the winter, the lake by our house froze, and we tied a nylon rope to the back of the dune buggy. At the other end, we attached a big tractor inner tube. We'd put two or three of the kids in the inner tube and tear that dune buggy down across our driveway and out onto the lake, whipping the thing around once we hit the ice. We'd be going so fast, that if you weren't completely down inside the inner tube, the force of the spin would throw you right out of it. You talk about some fun! Bonnie, on the other hand, wasn't so happy about it.

You see, I bought it for Christmas, but Bonnie was sure that the kids were going to get hurt with it. "No, no," I said. "I'll show 'em how to drive it." Of course, this thing had roll bars on it, seatbelts and everything, so there wasn't really any way that you could get hurt in it even if you turned the whole thing over. Well, the first day we had it, Christmas Day, the ground was frozen, and I drove it out in the fields to show the kids how you could do three-sixties and all that kind of stuff in it. I went tearing out across the field and started into a three-sixty, but there was a little ditch in the field about nine inches wide and four inches deep, and when the buggy was sliding sideways it dropped down in that ditch and started to flip. Now, I had the seatbelts and everything on, but my natural reflex was to stick my arm out to catch myself. If I had just kept my arm inside everything would have been fine, but my arm acted like a pole-vault stick, and me, the dune buggy, and everything was on my arm and I flipped the whole thing over.

I hurt my elbow so bad, but there wasn't any way I could tell Bonnie, and I told the kids, "Don't you go mention this to Mom!" When we got in the house that night to eat dinner, I was sitting there with the fork in my hand, but I couldn't bend my arm. So, I had my elbow jacked up around my ear trying to eat that way, just reaching for the food. Bonnie saw me and barked, "What's the matter with you?" "Aw, nothing," I said, "It's my elbow. It's just sore or something. I don't know what it is." "You turned the dune buggy over, didn't you," she shouted. "Yeah, I turned it over," I admitted, and we had a nice long conversation about that. Our kids had a lot of fun on those four-wheelers, though.

My youngest son, Chuck, got involved with racing these four-wheelers, and he eventually bought a high-powered, hopped-up new one to race professionally with. He wasn't only racing the dirt tracks around the country, he raced in the Hoosier Dome, Riverfront Stadium, and Freedom Hall in Louisville. He was into big-time racing. Bonnie and I were really concerned that he was going to get hurt doing that, and we kept trying to talk him into quitting. It was always the same answer from him, though, "I know what I'm doing and I'm not going to get hurt." My answer to that was, "Sure, you know what you're doing, but does the guy who's going to land on top of you know what he's doing?"

Anyway, he kept racing, and when Chuck and Tracye got married, I tried to talk to him again. "Chuck, you're married. You've got a lot of new responsibility. You've got a wife and it's time for you to quit racing," but he still couldn't hear me. About a year later, their first baby came along. Bonnie and I went over to the hospital, and soon Chuck came out of the delivery room in his green hat, cover gown, and booties, holding his beautiful baby girl like a proud father. I looked down at that little girl, and then back up at Chuck, and said, "Boy, I just can't wait until I can get her on a four-wheeler!" He looked up at me and never said a word, but the next day he came home, loaded up his four-wheeler, took it to town and sold it.

Tragedy

There's one more thing that I'd like to share with you in this chapter. In everyone's life, things are never all "honey and pie," and it hasn't been that way for our family either. We've had three instances that have really been trying for us. Back when Kimmy was about fifteen, and Beverly was about thirteen, they wanted some horses. Well, I bought them some horses, Honey and Babe were their names. The first year, they rode and rode those animals, and they had a lot of fun. The second year, though, the fun kind of wore off, so I ended up having to saddle up the horses myself and I had to make those two ride them.

One day in February, it was one of those warm, gusty winter days, Kim and a friend of hers decided to go for a ride. They were on a county road and a gust of wind blew a piece of paper out in front of those horses. They hadn't been ridden for so long that they just spooked, and one of them ended up throwing Kimmy off. Her foot got stuck in the stirrup, and the horse ran and dragged her for a little bit. She banged her head pretty good, and her whole left side was rubbed bare. She laid in the hospital almost two days unconscious, but she came out of it, and when we got home from the hospital, those horses were sold. Beverly says yet today that if Kimmy knew how to ride a horse, she'd still have hers.

Then, about six years ago, when she was about a year and a half old, Louie and Katie's daughter Amy fell into a hot tub and almost drowned. My son Louie was going out to clean the hot

107

tub — it was in the summer — and he opened the gate to it so he could get in there and change some of its valves and such. Then, he had to walk around outside to get into his to his garage, where the pumps were, so that he could change some more valves. At that time, both his little girls, Abby and Amy, had followed him around the garage. When he came out from the garage, he saw Abby on her backyard play set, and she wanted to swing. So he stopped and played with her for a little bit, not realizing that Amy had already gone into the house. After about fifteen or twenty minutes, he walked into the house and saw Amy floating in the hot tub, blue as she could be.

When Amy was born, she had problems breathing while she slept, so Louie had learned how to give her infant CPR. They called an ambulance, but realized that Amy was so bad that there was no way they could wait for it, and Katie and Louie took her to Floyd Memorial Hospital themselves. She stopped breathing three times along the way between here and the hospital, which is about a fifteen-minute trip. At the hospital, they took one look at her, put her on oxygen, placed her in an ambulance, and drove her over to Kosair Children's Hospital in Louisville. She stayed in a coma for ninety two hours as all our family watched, waited, and prayed.

I never will forget the chaplain that was there. He'd come walking down the hall, look in the door to intensive care, and then he'd look down the hall at us. "Looking good, looking good," he'd say. "I believe she's going to be fine." Then, he'd come, get me by the arm, and take me around the corner. "I'll tell it to you straight, Mr. Huber, she's in bad shape." He said, "You know, there are things in life that are worse than death. She could come out of this as an absolute vegetable. Now, you don't need to be telling anybody this," and he shook his head as he said it, "but somebody needs to be aware of it." So then we'd go back around the corner, all smiles again. That was a long, long, ninety two hours.

One day, she started to stir a little bit, and the doctor said, "Pretty soon, she'll come to, and we'll know immediately whether she's all right or not." She did come to, and she reached out for her mother and whispered the word, "Mommy." The doctor told Katie to pick her up, hug her and put her on the floor. So, Katie did, and Amy walked away just as normal as anything. She's fine now, but that was a rough time.

In the first part of May of 1993, Joe's wife, Kathy, was

diagnosed with a brain tumor. After running an MRI and several other tests, the doctors over in Louisville came to the determination that it was inoperable. The thing to do, they said, was to go home, wait six months, and come back again. She was in the hospital about a week, and I told my son Joe, "You know, I don't like to play defense. It's no fun. I like to be on the offense, because if you are, you've got a little control. Let's play a little offense and see if we can get her in the Mayo Clinic."

We called them and they told us they were booked solid; that sometime in the next three months she'd call us back and let us know when she could come. Well, that was no good. Three months is too long when you've got a brain tumor that's growing. So, we prayed, and we prayed, and I started thinking, "Who do I know that can help me? Who can help me open the door to get her in?" So, I'm beating my head against a wall, making a list of all the people I could call who might be able to get her in sooner. The next morning at five minutes after eight, we got a call from the clinic telling us they had a cancellation and that they had an immediate opening if we could be there the next morning. God works in lots of ways.

We took her in, and three days later they did the surgery and removed the tumor. Luckily, Kathy had a hundred percent recision. That's been two years ago, and she is still as clean as a pin; she no longer has cancer there. She still has seizures, but she's starting to accept that, and there are certain limitations that she's learning to live with, but life is going on for Joe, Kathy and their children, and I think every day is a better day for her.

That's the reason my son Joe started the Starlight Day Lily Gardens. Kathy wasn't physically capable of doing our book-keeping anymore, and I think she felt bad that she couldn't continue to contribute. She withdrew into herself a little bit, and Joe came up with the idea of starting a small business where he, Kathy, and their children could get involved on a small scale. It was something they could do together as family. That's what the Day Lily Gardens are all about, and Kathy really enjoys it. Everybody has some adversity in their lifetimes, and we've had ours too, but when it comes, you turn to your God, and he'll help you through it. He has us.

Slowing down

Two years ago, Bonnie and I were trying to figure out a way we could slow down, how we could get out of the rat race. So, we had an opportunity to buy twenty acres of wooded land that had a house on it that was five years old. It also had a little cabin on it that was twenty by twenty eight feet. We decided it would be a nice place to buy to go hide in so that we could get out of the hustle and bustle, and that we could have as a place our family could spend some time alone in. Well, Bonnie and I are in the process of remodeling this home; we've put a great big deck on it so that all of our children and grandchildren can come back here, and we intend to have all of our family back there at least once a week for dinner, along with all the birthdays and other special occasions.

The little cabin that's back there we've remodeled with a new deck and a screen enclosure, and it's for Bonnie's sister Norma and her husband Carl to use as long as they like. Its kind of our way of saying thank you for everything that they did for all of us on all of our vacations to Florida. It's also a way for Norma to come up here and be with all her sisters. It's another way for family to help family.

Something that maybe a lot of people don't realize is that all five of our children have new homes built right here on our farm, and Bonnie and I have the opportunity to see our children and grandchildren everyday. The time that Bonnie and I get to spend hauling our grandkids around every night on the back of our golf cart is what the two of us consider quality time. Having all of our children's homes built here, and being able to see them all the time, is a great source of satisfaction for the both of us.

Recipe:

Barbecued Bologna

Slice bologna 1/4 inch thick and cut slits in the edges of the slices. Pour your favorite barbecue sauce on the bologna. Put under broiler in oven until brown. This is really good.

The Huber family today — kids, spouses, and grandkids. First row, from left, Amy, Abby, Terra, Samantha, and Brittany. Second row, Katie, Lucas, Lewis, Jr., Kathy, Jenna, Bonnie, Kim (expecting the twefth grandchild), Clinton, Tracye, and Beverly. Standing, Lewis (Louie), Joe IV, Joe III, Joe, Mike, Chuck, Kenny, and Jason.

10

Visions for the Future

A lot of the things that get done around here come about just from listening to people. Bonnie and I have been doing this for twenty-eight years, and we've always tried to listen to the people who come to our farm because they tell us what they'd like to see, what they'd like to have. More and more, we're hearing about the educational and recreational side of the farm. People want a place where they can bring their kids to have fun and learn at the same time. Right now, we're tagging and putting names on everything we raise in the garden, so that people can look at the vegetables and know what they are. That's something people like. Long after Bonnie and I are gone, our family will still be providing services that other folks and their families can enjoy, simply because we try to listen to people and give them what they want.

I think another thing we'll probably start pointing out more on our farm — which has always been a way of life with us even though we really haven't pointed it out much in the past — is how much we do for the environment. Since 1843, when our family first moved to Starlight, we've been some of the biggest environmentalists you could find. On our farm today, any place that the land can erode is planted with apples, blackberries, raspberries, something where you can have grass sod in there so that the land can't wash away. We're building a beautiful new landscape park on the east side of the restaurant that will have wildflowers, plants, and day lily gardens. We've planted eleven different kinds of trees in there, not only to educate people and their kids, but to help preserve the land, because this piece of land slopes and tends to wash if we get a hard rain. If we get some grass down and make an

113

attractive park, it not only serves the people but it helps the land, too. It's part of this "Earth Day" movement, and I think we're going to try to emphasize that a little bit more around here so that we can educate people as to what everybody can do to try to take care of the land.

People don't come up here just to learn. They also come up here for recreation, so we've got to continue to come up with new ways for people to entertain themselves while they're with us. Because they really seem to enjoy picking their own apples, strawberries, and the like, I believe that we're going to spend a little more time expanding the fruits that we grow. In the fall, the number of people we get out here that want to pick their own pumpkins has grown every year, but for fall 1995 we've also developed an idea to plant a really large maze on about three acres of land. We'll be planting a special breed of corn in this area that grows about ten feet tall, and after it's grown up we're going to take a tractor and a mower to mow enough trails through it to get you lost. We're planning to plant it thick enough so that you won't even be able to see to the edge, but it'll be a fun thing, though, for families to walk through and get lost together in. That's something new that we're going to try that I think people will really enjoy.

Our farm

A couple made a comment to Bonnie not long ago that really made her day and mine, too. They said, "You know, a lot of people can't afford their own farm. When we come out here and walk around on your place, this is our farm." Now that's an awfully good feeling when we can have our customers come out and feel like this is their place. When Harvey Sloane was the Mayor of Louisville, he always referred to this as Louisville's farm, and he really felt strongly about that. We've got third generations coming here. I was talking to a family one Sunday up by the company picnic building, and the woman said, "Twenty-two years ago my husband and I first started coming over here with our kids, and now we've got our grandkids here with us today." It's just something this family does three or four times a year. Their whole family comes here. We'd like for our children to be able to continue the tradition of having our customers feel that our farm . . . is their farm.

Stepping back

Bonnie and I have always encouraged our kids to do what they enjoy with their lives. After our kids got out of college, we always pushed them to do other things. "Hey, go someplace else. Work a year some other place. If you decide you want to come back, great. We'd love to have you, but be sure this is what you want to do." All of them except Louie left the farm, because he always said this is where he wanted to be. I think it's awfully important that each individual has an opportunity to do what they want with their life. Chuck, for example, enjoys flying, and so he has his commercial pilot's license. When we have company picnics planned, he's right here because this is his number-one priority, but during the winter months, when things slow down, he has the opportunity to do a little freelance work as a pilot, and I think that it's pretty neat that things worked out like that.

Consciously, Bonnie and I have really tried to step back and let our kids take over the operations of the farm, because it's what they want to do. Bonnie and I have seen a lot of change over the last twenty-eight years. We went from a general farm, to a Pick Your Own farm, to a Pick Your Own farm with a farm market, which grew to a bigger farm market, and then the restaurant and the company picnic buildings came; so we've seen a lot. Over the last five years, though, we have really tried to step back. Who's going to fill our shoes? It's going to be our family. They already have done a superior job of stepping up and taking over, and they really work well together.

The secret of a family working well together is communication. You've got to be able to talk, and family meetings are the way to do that. When we have our family meetings, we always start them out the same way. We have a little prayer, and then I make this statement, "We're here to talk about business. We're not talking about personalities. If someone makes a suggestion to you in the area that you're managing and responsible for, you have to understand that they're not picking on you personally; it's just something that they've observed that they think will make you more efficient or that they think will make for a more enjoyable experience for the customer that comes here. It's constructive criticism. We're not picking on personalities here." Now, when you're a close family and you work with each other every day, you have to be able to talk. Everybody has to know what everybody else is thinking. Communicating is not only talking, it's also listening. You've got to be able to understand where the other person is coming from, and our children have the ability to do that with each other. Because they work so well together, it gives Bonnie and me opportunities to focus on other things.

People ask us if we think we're ever going to retire, and I always emphatically respond, "Yes!" Bonnie and I both intend to retire, but we both figure that we're really going to be involved with the P.R. around our place. People want to see Bonnie when they come out here. They want to talk to her. They're used to seeing both of us around here, and a lot them know us very well. They've been dealing with us for twenty-eight years, and we're friends. So, we're going to continue to be available to talk to people, but in our minds we think we're probably going to come floating in around 10:30 or 11:00 o'clock in the morning and stay through the lunch hour, and then we're going come back home to horse around until we decide if we want to head back up there in the evening or not. We can look down the reservation list and know who's going to be here or not. The people who've been coming here for years know to make a reservation, and there are certain people whom I can guarantee you that we *will* be there to see.

You have to understand that we enjoy it. We love to talk to people. If we didn't enjoy it we wouldn't worry about it. Bonnie has just been tremendous; people love to talk to her, and it sounds egotistical, but some of them enjoy talking to me, too. So, we see public relations as kind of our primary role, and I probably will continue to do the advertising, making the commercials and doing the little garden show. For a while, I'm sure that Bonnie and I will sit in on the family meetings, but not call the shots. We're hoping that our children will get all the facts and information together about their ideas, and if they ask us for our opinion, I'm pretty sure that we'll go along with whatever they decide. It's kind of been like that the past four or five years anyway, and we hope we can continue to slow down.

Mac Davis had a song about fifteen years ago called "You've Got to Stop and Smell the Roses." There's a lot of truth in that song, and Bonnie and I hopefully are going to do just that. We haven't made any definite plans yet, but we think we'll probably travel a little bit — not a whole lot because we've already

116

done quite a bit of it. Over the past twenty years, we've been all over this country giving talks at marketing seminars and that type of thing; we've been to thirty-eight states and also to Canada six different times.

Young blood

Our grandkids really do take an interest in the farm. Something that lights us up is when we watch Katie's oldest daughter Abby walk through the restaurant pouring coffee. She's only twelve years old, and the people get the biggest kick out of seeing her; they say "There's Joe and Bonnie's granddaughter walking through here pouring coffee!" She does it because she enjoys it and she's taking an interest in the farm.

Little Joey — well, he's not little Joey any more; he's twenty years old — but I guarantee you if given a responsibility, he'll accept it. He'll do it and do it right. Because our grandchildren are already doing so much, I have no doubt in my mind that they'll come in and take over. That's the only way that this farm will continue to prosper, because it's the young blood that's willing to come in and make the changes. Change is going to come, and young people can accept and make the changes a whole lot easier than people in my generation can. You reach the point in life when it just becomes normal to resist change. "Hey, everything's fine. What do you want to change it for. It's fine!" That's not the real world, though. In the real world, everything changes and you have to be able to adapt. I knew five or six years ago that it was time for us to let our kids start calling the shots, because we were starting to resist change, and that's no good; but I have no doubt that our children and grandchildren will step up and make the changes necessary to keep this farm successful.

Bonnie and I were married forty-one years as of May 1, 1995, and all the time we've been raising our children, we have really strived to teach them to accept responsibility for their actions. We have talked to them about the values of life and about our family values. I have this philosophy, and I've said it lot's of times: "The only thing you get out of life is what you do for somebody else." That's something Bonnie and I have tried to live by for our family, our community, and our church, and we've tried to live by it in doing something for every customer that has come to our farm. I believe if you can keep in mind that

117

what you're doing is for somebody else, you'll be successful; and I believe that whenever you get self-centered and start to worry about "me" before you worry about "we," you're going to get in big trouble. I think our children have that same philosophy. So if you're wondering what we'll do to prepare our children to take over the farm, just realize that we've already been preparing them for forty-one years.

Retired life

I think now that we're going to have a little more free time, we might try do be a little more actively involved with our family, community and church, but that's hard to say because we've always tried to be actively involved in all of those areas. I guess my goal right now is to continue to do what I've tried to do all my life, and that's help other people. My mother was ninety-four years old when she passed away, and her whole life was dedicated to trying to help other people. When we were at the funeral home, we wondered how many people would come to see her. "Mother's ninety-four years old, her friends are all gone." I've been in funeral homes when elderly people have passed away, and other than the absolute immediate family, there wasn't anybody there. Nobody! Five or six other people might stop in, but when my mother passed away it was a solid stream of people for eighteen straight hours, nine hours on Monday and nine hours on Tuesday. The cards are still coming, and the flowers . . . It was unreal, but they were there because Mother had touched their lives. She touched so many people, and that just proved to me once again, "The only things you can do in your life that are worthwhile are the things you do for other people," so I'll probably try to do more of those things once I retire.

Bonnie is kept so busy that she probably can't even imagine what else she'll get into, but one thing I know that she would like to be able to do is have the family get together one evening a week for dinner. Before we built the restaurant, we always got together every Sunday for dinner. After it was built, though, we got so busy that it hasn't happened since. We just didn't have the time to do it. I've already heard her make the comment that she wanted to start getting the family back together for dinner, and if Bonnie can find the time to fix it, surely everybody else can walk away for just the little bit of time it takes to eat it.

We've also talked about planting ourselves a little twelve-by-twelve garden out here so that we can have our little green onions, our little red radishes, and our lettuce in the spring of the year; maybe two or three tomato plants and a couple of pepper plants, kind of like the guy in town grows in his backyard. Something that we can just go out there and pick, and hopefully we can do it really, really good so that we can tell the boys up on the farm, "Hey, look at my garden," or show it to our grandkids. That'd be the biggest kick, I think, to say, "Look at Grandpa's garden. Have you got the farm looking like this, Little Joe?"

The only problem we'd have planting a little garden, though, is that we'd probably have to fence it in because the deer will eat it up out here, and keeping the squirrels out is really a challenge, too. The greatest thing Joe Huber has ever had going for him is all the people that lived in the city who grew their own gardens and knew what fresh vegetables tasted like. Their only problem was that they'd have squirrels eat their garden up every year. Those people love fresh vegetables, but they have to come out here to get them. The squirrels and the rabbits that eat up people's gardens have always been the best friends I've ever had!

Getting back on track, though, family always has been, and always will be our number one priority. Hopefully, when Bonnie and I can get really serious about retiring, we'll be able to spend more time with our grandchildren. We may start taking them to the volleyball and basketball games, that kind of thing. We really haven't had the opportunity to do that yet because we've been to "dag-gone" busy, but hopefully we can get more involved with our grandkids as time goes by.

A final word

I guess a simple word of advice for the following generations in my family would be, "Follow your roots" — what we've talked about through this whole book, starting back with my great-great grandfather, and on down through my mom and dad, my brothers and sisters, Bonnie's family, Grandpa Koetter; the values that all those generations of people had, the moral values, the family values, they've been passed on to us, and we've done our best to pass them on to you. One of the major goals that Bonnie and I will have is passing the family values

119

on to our grandchildren, and hopefully we'll be around long enough to pass on a little to our great-grandchildren too. The way society is going today, this whole nation has got to come back to family and moral values. It has to get turned around! It has to! It's the only way that not only this nation, but this whole world is going to survive.

It's been my experience in life that whatever you do for somebody else just feels better than anything else. It feels good to help people. I've said for years and years that someday I'm going to preach a sermon, "Let me love you." In the house where I grew up, my mom and dad always preached, "Love one another! Love one another! Love your brothers and sisters! Do unto others as you would have them do unto you" — the golden rule. We heard it from our parents. We heard it from all of our teachers in school. We all hear our ministers in our churches on Sunday, "Love one another." There have been many times in my life, and everybody's experienced this, that I would have liked to help somebody, and do something for them, but their pride got in the way and they wouldn't let me. You say, "Let me do this for you," and they'll say, "No, no, don't do that," but I want to do it because I love you. People have to start letting "each other" love "one another." How can you sit there and love somebody if they won't let you? If we could instill that into all our grandchildren, that would absolutely be the best heritage that we could ever leave to our family. What else is there?

Recipe:

Homemade Ice Cream

6 eggs

1 14 oz. can Eagle Brand
  milk

2 pints whipping cream

2 tbsp. vanilla

2 pinches salt

2 cups sugar

whole milk

2 cups cut up peaches or
  strawberries (optional)

Mix first six ingredients. Pour into ice cream freezer. Add fruit, if using, then add milk to line of freezer. Mix well and cover. Fill freezer, alternating 2-inch layers of ice and 1/2 cup rock salt until full. Freeze.

St. John Church, Starlight, Indiana.

11

Thoughts from Others

T he following is reprinted with permission from W. Bruce Bell as it originally appeared in the Borden *Ban-ner-Gazette,* Sept. 2, 1976.

More important than you thought

One day at the age of 11 or 12, I came across an irresistible offer in the Youth's Companion magazine: sell 50 imitation oil paintings at 10 cents each and as a premium receive a four-bladed Barlow pocket knife — a utility I'd longed for but could never afford. Dad paid us boys the regular rate of five cents a gallon for picking strawberries, but those funds always vanished in Gill's Grove at Pekin on the Fourth.

After school and on Saturdays that winter I tramped across the snowy fields peddling colorful religious subjects and still lifes to kindly neighbors, and every sale brought me closer to the coveted prize. At last, only two pictures remained — a flowery study of Saint Cecelia at the organ, and a mouth-watering arrangement of grapes and watermelon — their appeal considerably marred by having spent the winter being unrolled, picked over, rejected and wrapped up again.

The sap was rising in the trees, and the need of a pocket knife to cut hickory whistles had become urgent when on a raw spring morning I set out to solicit Annie Huber, a devout Catholic and widowed mother of nine, who had worked, managed and prospered on her small farm.

Her two eldest sons, Nace and Bill, eventually parlayed a snub-nosed International pickup and a few local hauling jobs into the giant trucking firm, Huber and Huber. Before they sold the business a few years ago, you never traveled far on the Chicago-Louisville-Knoxville highway without meeting one of their big orange-colored semis, lettered in black. And as for employment at good pay, Huber and Huber was to Starlight what Col. Sanders has been to Henryville. At the time I'm writing about, Nace and Bill were still in knee pants.

As I plodded over the thawing ground that long-ago morning, I was struck with the dismal thought that if Mrs. Huber consented to buy a picture it would still leave me with one tattered remnant that nobody was likely to want. Mother had bought my first picture, and Dad might have given me the dime I would need, but I had been advised in the beginning that it was my decision and my responsibility.

After coming so near, I'd probably never own a Barlow knife. My eyes suddenly felt moist and I told myself it was the stinging wind.

Mrs. Huber studied the pictures. She seemed not to notice the smudges and the dog-eared corners. She said, "What a brave boy you were to walk two miles in the cold wind. You know, these colors are so pretty, I can't decide. I believe I'll just have to buy both pictures."

I never whittled an arrow or cut a hickory whistle without feeling a surge of gratitude for people like Mrs. Huber.

Many years have passed, but in my memory Annie Huber still outranks any heroine I knew in history or childhood fiction. Beset as she must have been with the problems of her own large family, she nevertheless could spare twenty cents, a few minutes of her time, and a word of praise for a neighbor's child. That one act of kindness — natural to her, and merely an incident in a busy day — was more than a Godsend to a small boy. It has had a lifetime effect on a man's way of thinking.

That's why I'm a pushover when the students come around selling magazines, fruit cakes, candles, Grit, greeting cards, flower seeds, or ball-point pens. My dollar (or yours) may be the final one needed to send the High School Band to perform in Florida, or enable some Senior to make that once-in-a-lifetime trip to New York with the class — the genesis of happy memories that may endure for half a century.

Maybe it's more important than you thought.

Joe III: on motivation

I don't know how to put this. I mean it's not like it's a "great big deal." It's put on by the local V.F.W. It's not any big deal at all. But, a fellow with them contacted me and said, "Every year we always give an award for the Citizen of the Year of Southern Indiana, and I don't understand why you have never nominated your mom or dad." I said, "Well, quite honestly, I don't think that would be my place to nominate my own parents for something like that; that'd be like blowing your own horn." He put me in my place real quick because he pointed out that there's probably nobody else around that knows more of all that those two have done. He pretty much demanded that I nominate both of my parents, and he went on to say that he hoped it would be the first time that the V.F.W would have a tie.

I told him I'd think about it and get back in touch with him, and quite honestly, I was hoping that he'd just go away; but three or four days later he called me back wanting to know if I had all the information that he needed for their nomination. I started making excuses about why I hadn't gotten anything together for him and he cut me off. "Look," he said, "I'm serious about this. They're going to be nominated, and I would like it to be by you, because you have all the information about what they've done!" So, I agreed and I started making calls to try and get all the material together.

Naturally, I realized that my dad was involved in a lot of things, but when all this information started coming in, I've got to tell you, it was mind-boggling. I hadn't realized myself all that man was involved in. I did know about some of the things, but even then, I didn't know the extent that he was involved with them. For example, I knew that he was on the Board of Directors of the R.E.M.C., but I didn't know about all of its other committees that he served on. I knew he was on the Board of Directors at the bank, but I didn't know that he served on the Trust Committee, and I didn't know he was the Chairman of the Loan Committee. The list just went on and on and on.

I called the people in Washington, DC, to get the information about when he served on the Finance Committee of the C.F.C. (Corporate Finance Corporation), which is basically a bank that lends money to Rural Electric Corporations all across the United States. The only mention that Dad ever made about being on the C.F.C. is when he was on a committee that built a new

125

building up there. Now, I don't know all the specifics of it, because he'll never tell anybody any of this stuff, but his name is on a plaque inside that building as one of the charter members.

I stopped and thought, "How did he run this farm and do all that other, too?" I don't think I would have been able to ever find the time to do the other part alone. I always asked him, "Why do you do all that stuff?" and he always responded, "Well, the good Lord's been awful good to me; this community and the Louisville metropolitan area's been awful good to me, and I just feel like I ought to give something back." When he was fifty, I asked him again, "Look, you've done your part. You've done more than enough. Why don't you slow down and enjoy life?" That time he responded by saying, "I've got to stay out of you boys' way. When I took over my dad's farm, I never felt free to really take over and do my own thing. As my dad got older, he became more resistant to change, and I don't want that to happen to you. You guys have got to learn to take on the responsibility, because someday, I hope, this business will be yours. If I'm not here, it forces you to call the shots. And another thing, don't get the wrong idea; I enjoy this." It got to be kind of a joke between my brothers and me: "When's Dad going to be leaving? Next week? Good, because we need to get caught up!" Dad had the right idea, and I didn't realize it at the time, but he was watching our backs, and we were watching his, and that continues even today.

I know the guy pretty well, and I know he'll back away from running things, but retiring for him is going to more difficult than it is for a lot of people. When he retires, what's going to happen is he's going to stop getting a paycheck from this company, and other than that, not much is going to change. He'll let us go, but I know that from somewhere out in the distance, he's going to be watching our backs. He has to. He worked awfully hard to build what he did and he's not going to let me and my brothers foul it up.

Nobody knows how hard he and my mom worked to get this place. I can remember when I was growing up how those two were very conservative about spending any money. They didn't believe in going to the bank and borrowing money for operating capital or to buy a tractor. If they didn't have the money, they made do with what they had. It was that simple. That was their philosophy. They worked, they saved their money, and they didn't squander it away. At the end of the year, if there was money left, they'd decide what they needed the most, and what would help them turn a profit on this farm. It wasn't what they wanted, it was what they needed that they got. Don't ask me why, but sometimes it seems that he's almost embarrassed when he looks out around this farm and remembers how long it took him to build it up to what it is today. He's remarked that if he was a good business manager they could have probably built this up in three or four years, but they took the conservative route. A lot of people don't take that route, and a lot of people are bankrupt, too. There's a trade-off, but when more money became available, they became more aggressive, and that's when things started speeding up. He always said, "It's a lot easier to save a dollar than it is to make a dollar," and he was right.

He also always preached about taking care of the little things. "If you just take care of the little things, you don't have to worry about the big ones." He's done that with everything on this farm, from the tomato plants to the restaurant; he's always taken care of the little problems. It's a lot easier to fix a tomato plant in the early stage of a disease then it is when the disease is full blown. It's a lot easier to please the customers by taking care of their little problems then when they've got big ones. He'll drive himself crazy looking over the books trying to figure out why business was slow one day in May three years ago. Eventually he'll figure out that it was Derby Day, and then he'll be all right. I'll tell you, I don't know what drives and motivates that man, but I wish I had more of it in me.

Butch Kruer: on good people

Joe was the one that started this U-Pick business, and it took over like I don't know what. It took roots and grew like a house on fire. If you come out here in the summertime, when we've got strawberries to pick and greens to cut, pickles to pick and cantaloupes and pumpkins, you just wouldn't believe the traffic around here. During strawberry time, I can hardly even cross the road to get my mail, and the biggest part of the traffic around here comes from Louisville. But when Joe decided he was going to build that restaurant, I told him it'd be the biggest mistake he ever made in his life. I told Joe he'd never believe how much work there was to it, but he built it anyway, and he came out O.K.

It all goes back to one thing, though, treating people right. Joe and Bonnie both bend over backwards trying to treat people right. A couple of years ago, every Saturday and Sunday afternoon, they had a big tent outside with a band that played for four hours, from 1:00 to 5:00; and it cost Joe good money to have them play, but they also had a chuckwagon out there. Now, my wife and I used to come up Saturday evening just to hear the band play, because if you didn't want to spend any money on the food or beer, it didn't cost you a dime to listen to the music.

Every time my wife and I come up here, we never pay a dime. Joe's always telling them to put our meals on the Huber ticket; that's why we don't come over very much. We've gotten I don't know how many gift certificates for Joe Huber's Family Restaurant as gifts, and we can't use the things; Joe's always picking up the tab. I'd been carrying a $20 one around for as long as I can remember, and the last time I was up here, I just gave it back to Joe because he picked up the tab again. I just said, "Here! I'll be carrying this thing around for the rest of my life, and I want to get rid of it right now!" They treat everybody in this community right. Ask anybody around here, and they'll tell you what kind of people they are. If somebody needs help, Joe will be the first in line to help, and it doesn't matter what it costs him. That's the kind of guy he is.

Paul Huber: looking back

All the older ones in the Huber family play pinochle, and for a while, we always got together for an annual fishing trip. About twenty-five of us would go to Lake Barkley, or down to Knoxville or Alabama, and we'd fish during the day and in the evenings we'd have our pinochle games. We were in Alabama, staying in one of those old family-owned motels, nice place, and we had about half of it rented. We needed one large room to play pinochle in, because everybody wanted to be in the same room, but they didn't have any that size, so whoever set the trip up went across the road and rented an auctioneer's office that was big enough to put five or six tables in.

Well, we went fishing that day and went out to dinner that night, and after we got back, we went over to the office we had rented to play pinochle. So there we were, playing pinochle, and we looked up, and there were five deputy sheriffs in this room with us. Nobody saw them come in, nobody! They said they had complaints that we were drinking and gambling. One of us said, "There's not a drink in the house, and there's not a nickel on the table," and they just couldn't believe it. One of those deputies was so pumped up that he had a riot gun, and he was ready to do something! But his timing was premature. Later in the evening thirsts *were* quenched; and settlement is made at the *end* of a pinochle game.

Another thing that I'll never forget is the day our jersey bull got my dad down. I was sitting in the car, and I was getting ready to pull it into the shed. I saw Dad go up to get that bull in, and I looked down to start the car up. When I looked back up, all I saw was a big cloud of dust, and I knew something was wrong. I got excited and jumped out of the car to run to the house and get Dad's shotgun, and when I got the up to the field, Dad was sitting on the roadside with blood all over him. He growled, "Give me the gun," and he raised up and shot the bull. Of course, he was far enough away that he just stung him, and the bull ran down to the barn. Then Dad told me to give him another shell. I asked him what he was going to do, and he said, "I'm going to go put that 'so and so' in the barn." "You can't do that," I replied, but he climbed up over the fence and he went down through the field anyway. When he did, that bull came running back and met him about halfway. Dad held back until that bull got close to him, and then raised up and shot him in the knee. Well, the bull went down, and so did he. There laid the bull, and there laid Dad.

We got Dad to the hospital, and it was touch and go there for a little bit; and the next morning, Mother said that the bull was going to the market. Now, that night, one of my uncles decided that they better go check on the bull, because they all had visions of the bull laying out there bleeding to death, but when they drove out into the field in their car, the bull chased the them out of the field, so they decided that the bull was all right. I'll always remember the next morning, I was picking pickles and looked up and saw this "army" walking across the field to get that bull. One of them had a shotgun, another one had a baseball bat, one of them had a pitchfork, and one of them had a grubbing hoe. They picked up anything they could. They also had one of my uncle's shepherd dogs with them and, the truth be told, that dog is the one who the got the bull in the barn. The men couldn't handle him because he was too big and mean, but the dog would just grab on to the bull's tail and nip him in the ankles a little bit, and he finally got him in the barn. Then they got about six ropes around his neck and got him on the truck to take him to market. We never had mean bulls after that.

Larry: little things that mean a lot

Looking back to my childhood days, I recall many little things that Joe did to make my life a little better. Joe was the person that somewhat looked out for me when I was younger, and he helped me out quite a bit. I remember when I was in the first grade and a little nervous about going to school. Joe would go out to the apple orchard and pick the biggest apples he could find for me to take to school to Sister Doris, the first-grade teacher. We continued to do this for the first few weeks of my first grade year, and Sister Doris took a liking to me and those big apples.

Also in the first grade Joe helped me out when I got myself in a little bind. At the beginning of the year we didn't have any homework, and I got used to not bringing my books home. Well, when I got my first homework assignment I completely forgot to bring my books home, and I was pretty upset. Joe came in from working and saw that I was pretty out of shape, and he asked, "What's the matter with you?" I responded, "I left my books at school and I have a homework assignment to turn in tomorrow." Joe took it upon himself to go to Sister Doris's home and see if she would let me get my book. Well, she went right over to the school, unlocked it, and got my books and gave them to Joe. He thanked her and said, "I think Larry will never forget to bring his books home again." And after that, I never did.

Joe showed responsibility when it came to the family eating together. I remember that, as we gathered at the table to eat dinner, Joe was always in the middle of the table. While he sat there, food was moving from one end to the other pretty quickly. Joe would be right there in the middle just relaying the food back and forth. The result was that he didn't find much time to eat for himself. He always said that his sitting there in the middle of the table kept him a thin young man.

Joe also was the person who was in charge of getting the younger kids' Easter baskets ready. It was a tradition that we would go out to the wooded knobs around here, gather up some of the moss, and use it as the Easter Bunny's nest. Early on Easter morning we would get up and go see what the had been left in the nest. One Easter I woke up pretty early, and when I went out to the nest I saw Joe with bags and boxes, filling our nest. As soon as he saw me, he quickly said, "Look at these bags and boxes the Easter Bunny left us!" not showing a bit of doubt. He always has been pretty quick on his feet.

He has a great sense of humor, too. At weddings here in Starlight, the tradition is to pull a mischievous trick on the bride and groom before they leave to go on the honeymoon. Well, at my sister Bitsy and her husband Pat's wedding we planned something good. The wedding went real smooth and Bitsy began to wonder if we were going to play a prank on her or not. It came to the point where they were leaving to go on the honeymoon, and Pat was going to wear his suit and give Joe his tux to return. Well, he looked everywhere for that suit and couldn't find it, so Joe started helping him look all over the house searching for that suit. Pat never even noticed that Joe was wearing the suit, until my aunt finally made Joe tell Pat to look at what he had on. I'll never forget Pat's face when he realized that Joe had his suit on.

Finally, let me say this about Joe and Bonnie. You will never find better hosts than they are when it comes to family. We have been coming back to the farm, as a family, for a long time. No matter what is going on, Joe and Bonnie will take time out to be with our family. That's the way they are, and I believe that's why they have done so well. Thanks, Joe and Bonnie, for sharing time with us.

Kimmy and Beverly: on little brothers and free publicity

When we were young and if we got in trouble, we would definitely get a spanking, but more than that there was a lot of "Wait till your father gets home." That was Mom's big thing, and the anticipation of waiting until our father got home was really about enough to take care of it. One time, though, before Chuckie was born, one of us kids had gotten into Mother's lipstick, and Dad lined us up from biggest to littlest: Jo Jo, Kimmy, Beverly, and Louie. "Who did it?" he asked. Well, nobody confessed to it, so then he went down the line like a drill sergeant.

"Jo Jo, did you do it?"

131

"No."

"Kimmy, did you do it?"

"No."

"Beverly, did you do it?"

"No."

"Louie, did you do it?"

"No."

Because nobody 'fessed up to it, he decided that we were all going to get a spanking. Once again, he took us from biggest to littlest and Jo Jo got it, I got it, Beverly got it, and when it got down to Louie, he put his hands back, and there was the evidence: lipstick all over his hands.

I don't imagine there's anybody who's gotten as much free advertising as Dad has managed to get. I've been on the talk shows a couple of times because Mom didn't like to do it. I'd be on the morning shows with Dad talking about how to make Mom's short cake and jellies and the like. Everybody else hates to be in the public eye, but Dad does not have a bit of a problem with it. I believe Dad's excellent rapport with the local news media has a great deal to do with his level of success. He always said, "If you treat people right, all you need do is ask for help and you will get it." Dad certainly knows how to utilize his resources — from the news media to the time I took produce to Cincinnati "on a date."

Beverly recalls being on one of these interviews when she was fifteen: They asked everybody else nice, normal questions: "What's your age? What's your job," peaceful, family talk show questions. Then it got to me and I get, "What do you like to do on your dates?" The only thing I could think of to respond was, "Just anything to get away from here," and Dad about died.

Chuck: on flashlights

I came home from Purdue University in 1982, and, man, I couldn't wait to get out of that place. *My* teacher was my father, and the education I got from him taught me all about how to treat other people. He never really sat us down and talked to us about how to treat people right; he just led by example. The most important three things I learned from him are: you've got to treat people right; you've got to do the right thing; and the customer is always right. We may not always want to believe those things, but 99.9 percent of the time, they're true. When

I go into job interviews, I tell them, "The only education I've got came from my father," and they always tell me that's the best kind of education to have.

Another thing that I learned real quick when I was a teenager was that I needed to carry a flashlight with me when I went out at night, because Dad's big thing was that he'd rearrange all the patio furniture if I'd stayed out too late. Then I'd come sneaking in around two in the morning and BAM! I'd walk right into the loudest thing out there, knock it over, and then he'd know what time I got in. I soon got wise to that, though, and bought myself a little flashlight to take with me.

Charles Engle: on good neighbors

I grew up right here in Starlight, and the Hubers and I have been neighbors all my life. That whole bunch is a good family. Joe works hard, his family works hard, they work well together, and they're very helpful people, which is commendable. If anybody needs help some time, Joe's right there. We've always helped each other a lot, and we've got an excellent relationship because the Hubers are excellent neighbors. Our sons, years ago, helped him on his farm by driving trucks and delivering produce, and a big thing that sticks out in my mind is that a few years back he built a dam up on his farm in order to build a lake. Well, about half of the lake extends over the boundary onto our farm. So, in doing that, he also made an improvement to our farm. This whole community is like that because we help one another out whenever possible. There's never been a time, back through the years, when one of us needed help that the other one wasn't right there; we've used each other's tools and farm equipment. Being neighbors has just been a very rewarding experience for both of us.

Katie Huber: on success

When people come up here and don't see Joe, it's so funny the comments that you hear from them. "Oh, well, he's a millionaire, he's probably off running around in the Bahamas or somewhere." Little do they know he's right outside, digging in the dirt! But they only say that because he's always here and they're used to seeing him. I mean, for him to miss a day in here, there has to have been a death somewhere. More and more, though, we're having to encourage him and Bonnie to do other things; to go away and relax a little bit.

He's so smart and so successful, and I really don't know what it is about him that makes him that way. I think its just his voice. I mean, have you ever heard his commercials? He has the kind of voice that just makes people want to trust him. Everybody talks about it. They might not even hear a word he's said in those commercials, but inside they're saying, "I know that voice. That's Joe Huber. I like him." It's just amazing that he has so much knowledge about people and things without ever getting a college education. Borden High School back then was nothing compared to what it is today, but you can ask Joe anything, anything in the world, and he knows the answer. It's truly amazing. I'd love to be like that.

Tracye Huber: on friends and dreams

If there's one thing that everybody here agrees on, it's that we all want to make people happy. We try to give that little, extra personal touch that you can't always get at every other place. Whereas at some other place you just might be treated like an ordinary customer, over the years the people who come here have become our very good friends. A lot of the customers have seen Katie and me go from just getting married to having our kids, and a bunch of them bring birthday presents for our children. You don't get that just anywhere, and when we lose a customer due to death or something, we're losing a really good friend. Many of these people have known Bonnie and Joe since they started their little deal on the side of the road, and that's really something special.

One more thing needs to be said here. Our customers have been very good to us. They're very faithful, and everyone appreciates that. A lot of what we do here is trial and error, and since they're always the first ones to try something, we always trust their opinions on it. They've supported everything that we've done, and for that we thank them.

I also think that if everyone in the family continues to work and dream, like Bonnie and Joe do, this farm will always be here. I think it has a lot to offer to every person, whether they be single or married, have children or not. This place grows on dreams, and we've all got those. Anyone can see their dream come true if they're willing to work for it, and nowhere is that more true than on this farm. Bonnie and Joe I admire tremendously because this place is their dream, and they have given their whole lives to make something special here.

Chuck and I have two children, and we definitely want them to be able to experience what we've been able to, but just like Bonnie and Joe felt with their kids, we want this to be a place where they feel they want to be, and not a place they feel they have to be. This place is a dream come true for me because I get to work and be at home with my kids; not many working mothers get a chance to do that.

Fred Wiche: making it happen

I have always been told that raising peach trees is a rich man's hobby, and I found out that was true. I decided that I would put in fifty peach trees at the farm. However, I didn't have much experience in raising peaches, and I failed to thin the orchard out as the trees began to bear fruit. A storm happened to come through, and it damaged some of the trees. So, as I went on the air that morning, I talked about the damage to the trees. Joe was listening that morning, so he and Bonnie decided they would help me out. Listening to Joe through the years, I've heard him say "You've got to make it happen" many times, and when I came home they were at my farm with a bunch of duct tape, ready to fix those broken limbs. Now, I never asked for their help, but they came over because of my distress call. Without their help, we probably would have lost that entire crop, but they "made it happen," even though it did look a little weird.

Another morning I was on the air with Wayne Perkey and Ken Schulz when we started discussing some off-the-wall things, just going back and forth. Ken mentioned a birthday card he had received that said: "I've got good news and bad news. The good news is I got you a new car! The bad news is that it's stuck to the ceiling of your garage with peanut butter!" Ken continued this conversation by saying, "That would be like eating peanut butter pie. You couldn't eat it because it would stick to the roof of your mouth." "I quickly responded, "You can eat peanut butter pie!" Ken asked, "Where?" I told him that Joe Huber had peanut butter pie at his restaurant. I don't know if he believed me or not, but we continued with the regular program.

135

Joe heard our conversation, got a peanut butter pie from the restaurant, and brought it to the studio. Well, he found us, and we went on the air talking about eating the peanut butter pie he had brought us. It seemed like we spent most of that morning discussing peanut butter pie with people who called in asking about it. The thing about that situation was that Joe didn't have to come over here, but he did it because he wanted to make something happen. You have to admire someone like that who takes time out to show that special interest. Joe's bringing that pie over reflects how he has lived his life: he makes things happen.

Father John Beitans: on good will

Joe in a way is the soul of the community here. He's a person who has a vision of what a community like this should be, especially the ideal of people helping each other. What he has done is put that into practice, personally, every chance he's had. There's never a time when somebody mentions a need in passing, that he doesn't immediately respond, in even some small way that he can be helpful. It's just part of his philosophy of life, and it's just the way that he fulfills it; and he never fails. I've never heard him in any type of casual conversation to miss an opportunity.

They get into some major things too, like when a neighboring farmer has a threat of freezing coming up. Joe has some irrigation pipes that they can use for that process where they spray water on things just before they freeze in order to preserve them; he'll be there, and he'll do that. In fact, even his son Joe is the same way. A while back, we had some yucca plants in our cemetery that were tearing up the tombstones, and all I did was just go to Joe III for some advice about how to deal with them. He just said, "Don't worry about it. I'll take care of it," and by the time I'd left the restaurant and run some errands, he'd already sent his men out to spray them, and just like that, it was done. In other words, the job was finished before I got home myself, and all I'd done was ask for advice. There was never a word about inconvenience or cost, but the Hubers are known for that.The Huber family have done it consistently enough and long enough that everybody in the community knows they're that kind of people. Joe Huber has, you know, a hundred million dollars of good will.

Another good character trait that I see is this. We have several businesses up here that are what you would call competitive. Joe has a farm restaurant; the Stumlers have a farm restaurant; the Winery, in a sense, has a farm restaurant; but these people do not see each other as the "enemy." They're constantly over at each other's places and doing anything that they can for each other. It's not just Joe, it really is part of this community; but this community wouldn't be the community that it is unless its most visible citizens clearly embodied what the community is supposed to be. The visible is so clear that it serves as a model and guide for everybody. It's good for the church that's here; its good for everybody.

Joey Huber: taking over

My grandfather's big thing is being efficient. You have to be efficient all the time, because if you are, it takes a lot less time, you don't have to go back and do it again, and it saves a lot of money. "Do it right the first time and be efficient when you do it." You don't need ten guys doing something that only takes two to do. He's also preached and preached to me, "It's not the big things you've got to make happen, it's all these little things. If you make the little things happen, the big things will do themselves." The "correct way," I've learned, is "his way."

Now, I don't know about the farm itself, but I think my two sisters will be involved up here somewhere. I'm drawn to the farm because I love the outdoors; seeing everything grow, and knowing that I'm doing it. I'm running the packing shed now, but I'm sure he'll keep moving me up, and that one day I'll be running the farm by myself, because, as everyone knows, my grandfather's getting ready to retire, and my dad's probably going to take over his position running the business. Eventually, after I learn what I'm doing, I'd like to fill his shoes.

The tradition goes on.

Recipe:
Chocolate Peanut Butter Pie

3 egg yolks
1 cup sugar
1 tsp. vanilla
1/4 cup cocoa
1/4 stick butter
1 baked pie shell

2-1/2 tbsp. cornstarch
2 cups milk
1/2 tsp. salt
1 cup powdered sugar
1/2 cup peanut butter

Meringue

3 egg whites
pinch salt
1/8 tsp. vanilla

3 tbsp. sugar
1/2 tsp. cream of tartar

Mix powdered sugar and peanut butter until crumbly. Cover bottom of pie shell. Mix sugar, cocoa, cornstarch, and salt and blend with egg yolks in bottom of double boiler. Add milk, butter, and vanilla and cook, stirring, over medium heat until thick. Pour over peanut butter mixture. Beat egg whites with salt and vanilla until stiff. Continue to beat in sugar and cream of tartar. Top pie filling with meringue, sealing edges. Bake at 325° until lightly browned.

To obtain additional copies of
Joe Huber: Winning with Family,
send check or money order for $12.95 each plus $3.00
each for shipping and handling to:

       Strawberry Press, Inc.
       P.O. Box 448
       Jeffersonville, IN 47131

Name ——————————————————————

Address ————————————————————

City ———————————— **State** —— **Zip** ————

Allow 3-4 weeks for delivery.

To obtain additional copies of
Joe Huber: Winning with Family,
send check or money order for $12.95 each plus $3.00
each for shipping and handling to:

       Strawberry Press, Inc.
       P.O. Box 448
       Jeffersonville, IN 47131

Name ——————————————————————

Address ————————————————————

City ———————————— **State** —— **Zip** ————

Allow 3-4 weeks for delivery.